Plugger

Rudy Grigar—"Plugger"—with a stringer of redfish and speckled trout caught at night on artificial lures in Christmas Bay, November 27, 1958. Grassy flats such as these are ideal for catching saltwater game fish when the tides are right.

Plugger

Wade Fishing the Gulf Coast

Rudy Grigar

Introduced and Edited by
W. R. McAfee

Texas Tech University Press

This book is typeset in Palatino and Casablanca Antique. The paper used in this book meets the minimum requirements of ANSI/NISO Z39.48-1992 (R1997). ∞

Book design by Rob Neatherlin
Jacket photo by Joe Doggett, courtesy of the *Houston Chronicle*

Printed in the United States of America

Library of Congress Cataloging-in-Publication Data
Grigar, Rudy, 1915–2001
    Plugger: wade fishing the Gulf Coast / Rudy Grigar ; introduced and edited by W. R. McAfee.
       p. c.m.
    Includes index.
    ISBN 909672-377-1 (cloth : alk. paper)
    ISBN 0-89672-510-3 (paper : alk. paper)
    ISBN 978-0-89672-510-2
    1. Surf fishing—Gulf Coast (U.S.) I. McAfee, W. R., 1942–
II. Title.
SH464.G84G75   1997
799.1'664—dc21

                         97-4128
                         CIP

    12 13 14 15 16 / 9 8 7 6 5 4

Texas Tech University Press
Box 41037
Lubbock, Texas 79409-1037 USA
800.832.4042
ttup@ttu.edu
www.ttupress.org

For Mary, my wife, the wild mermaid of the sea

Acknowledgment

My thanks to W. R. McAfee who, from notes I'd jotted down over the years, interviews, and research on specific subjects, drafted this book for me.

Foreword

Rudy Grigar is more than a plugger; he is a purist. He is retired, yet his legacy has inspired several generations of saltwater anglers. For more than sixty years, Grigar has carried a real style to the tide line, and he helped define the classic approach to speckled trout and redfish on the Gulf Coast. His school of fishing was wading and casting artificial lures—period. Boats were for transportation and live bait was for "potlickers." A bucket of shrimp simply was not an option when you fished with Grigar. It is not for nothing that he earned the name the Plugger. During the two decades that I shared tides with Grigar, I never knew him to deviate from this stance. Not once. We first fished together in the spring of 1973, during my first year as an outdoor writer with the *Houston Chronicle*. At the time, Grigar based his expeditions from a stilted bay house near San Luis Pass below Lower West Galveston Bay.

That first morning, a beautiful late-spring day of light south-easterly breeze and shimmering green water, he carried the game to a higher level. We ran his Whaler to a sand flat in the open bay surrounded by trenches of deep water. It was a place I never knew existed. Rafts of mullets milled and popped, sliding with the tide across the shin-deep bar. The current was so clear we could see the shadows of the wind riffles moving across the white bottom.

Grigar and I waded side-by-side, casting black-and-silver mullet-imitation plugs. By screwing the line-eye into the nose, he had modified them to track straight and run shallow. Back then, almost nobody threw plugs in water that "skinny."

But Grigar did.

Schools of speckled trout were roaming the flat, scattering the pods of mullet. We followed the action, sniping at flurries of nervous bait and drawing vicious strikes. Spray would kick as the silver-and-spotted tide-runners turned on the plugs. Several times, as the morning sun climbed higher, opening the window of visibility, I thrilled to see the gray silhouette of a trout race to my cast through the sun-dappled shallows. We strung fifteen or twenty trout, all between two and five pounds, a routine catch for the Plugger. I was astounded. To me, trout fishing had been an exercise in blind ambition, "chuck-and-chance" casting in chest-deep water, or perhaps soaking live shrimp in the deeper channels. I had no idea, no concept, that coastal wading could be such a high-visibility combination of finesse and intensity.

Grigar fished with class. He carried this style throughout the many trips and the different venues that we shared—Galveston, Port O'Connor and, ultimately, the Chandeleur Islands. The Chandeleurs were, I believe, his special place. That remote barrier strip of sand and shell off Louisiana and Mississippi suited his "step-ahead-of-the-crowd" drive. He kept moving on the map, as well as in the water, always reaching for an empty shoreline "working alive" with bait and "wall to wall" with speckled trout and redfish.

Wherever he waded, the Plugger was easy to recognize. He had a signature profile. He used a vicious side-arm delivery with a two-handed rod and had a distinctive way of cradling the long butt under his arm and pointing the tip straight down the line during the retrieve. Rather than jerking the rod tip up and down to impart stuttered action to the lure, he exercised a curious side-to-side "Rudy Flip." I never could do it worth a damn. I guess you either have it or you don't.

I never knew Grigar to fish with awkward or cheap gear. His casting tackle was clean and smooth and refined, and his shallow-water act was as polished in its own way as that of any dry-fly angler on a spring creek. This was in bold contrast to many of the clumsy efforts that exist even today in saltwater. Grigar used long, whippy rods and small, fast reels (narrow-frame Ambassadeurs and Shimanos, as I recall). He spooled with light lines and made long casts and seldom, if ever, backlashed. He was favored with uncommon stamina and could wade all day. Even as a white-haired elder of the tribe, he could steam off and leave young Turks half his age in his wake. Trust me.

He was a methodical wader, not particularly fast, but when you looked up, he would be way over there. And if he paused for long, you could bet he was on fish, a lone silhouette under a dipping, bending rod. All you could do was shrug and begin a chugging, forced march and hope to close the gap before the school dispersed. Or the old man caught them all.

Two lures among the many hundreds were standbys for the Plugger. They were the L & S Mirr-O-Lures and the gold and copper Johnson Sprite Spoons. Pared to one, he probably would pick the Sprite. A good fisherman can make a proper spoon run fast and shallow, slow and deep, always a tempting target for bay fish. It would not be an exaggeration to say that Grigar put his kids through school with a Johnson Sprite.

He claims to have caught more than one million pounds of game fish. Whatever the amount, it is prodigious. Yet Grigar became one of the first voices of catch-and-release on speckled trout and redfish. This was not just lip service. He enjoyed releasing fish; I watched him do it as early as the mid-70s, back when regulations on saltwater finfish stood between slim and none. He realized sooner than most that the Gulf had limits to the abuses inflicted by man.

As his memoir shows, the Plugger is opinionated on many subjects and has seldom been shy in voicing his stance. His fishing clients included CEOs, doctors, lawyers, and various sporting luminaries, but all had to undergo the scrutiny of the master and many stood humbled on barrier-island campgrounds. "Piece of junk!" Grigar would say, reviewing some high-powered customer's new reel. "Wouldn't have it in my box."

Predictably, not everybody loved the Plugger. Maybe it was professional jealousy, maybe it was personality conflict, but at times Grigar had his critics. But I suspect that even his loudest detractors would concede that he played a solid and uncompromised game on the tide line. He fished hard and well during the twenty years that we shared trips—and he already was past his prime. Staying power aside, it is enough to know that Grigar included among his level-wind disciples and comrades some of the very finest light-tackle anglers on the coast. The big names usually speak well of the Plugger.

His memoirs are "wall to wall" with information, but more than that, they are a valuable piece of fishing history. The Plugger is a Gulf Coast original and he made his mark with lures in shallow water. He shares within these pages the techniques and philosophies that have influenced thousands of anglers during an active career that spans more than half a century.

Joe Doggett
1997

Preface

This book is written for the new breed of saltwater sport fishermen—the lure fishermen—and their children. It's a personal tale of fishing the Gulf Coast the first half of the century and pioneering wade fishing lures at a time when everyone else was using cut bait. It's also a personal recollection about the Gulf Coast dating back to 1924 when our stock fish and game were as plentiful as the Native Americans had left it; a time when every creek, bayou, canal, river, and lake were "wall to wall" with fish and the water was pure and drinkable; a time our children will never really know.

These early days were the "game hog" days when there were no limits on wild game or fish; when fishermen like myself worked these areas with our rods and reels, catching millions of pounds of fish. Looking back now at those years, I have to admit that my friends and I are partly responsible for the end of this abundance.

This book contains material taken from my personal records, diaries, and logs as well as my collection of photographs. The most important source for this book, however, are my memories of fishing the Gulf Coast for over fifty years and guiding other sport fishermen on the Chandeleur Islands located off the coast of Louisiana during the last eighteen years of my career.

I think I can truthfully say a few sportsmen and myself helped raise saltwater wade fishing from a hobby for a few enthusiasts into a sport that thousands enjoy today. We began by designing and manufacturing our own lures. Back then, wade fishing lures—and lures in general—were not manufactured on the scale they are today. Only the Johnson Silver Minnow, a small variety of silver spoons, and a few top-water baits were being produced; and these mainly for fresh-water fishing. Plus, they were hard to find; especially among saltwater fishermen. Consequently, we were forced to invent our own bait, adapting everyday objects or whittling from wood those lures we hoped would catch "the big one."

In this book there are a lot of people to recognize, both for their expertise and sportsmanship on the water, who, like me, helped pioneer Gulf Coast wade fishing. Besides Pluggin' Shorty and Doug English, I would also like to mention sportswriter Bob Brister of the *Houston Chronicle*, who incidentally, is the only survivor of our original group of saltwater lure fishermen besides myself. Others from those early days, who have passed on, include Zollie Taliaferro, "Captain" June Beckley, Louis Kasmoraski, Elmer Hawkins, Felix Stagno, St. Clar Brittian, and the Bullard Brothers. Others came later, adding to our ideas and knowledge: Bill Norman, Jack Sillman, Jack Emott, Bubba Silva, and Harold Reynolds. No one ever had to drag bottom to catch bait for any of these fishermen. They were lure purists all.

But enough about the past. Let me tell you a couple of reasons why I've loved to wade fish all these years—it's the greatest way in the world to stay in good physical condition and have fun while you're doing it!

At eighty I'm still in good physical shape, and I attribute it all to wade fishing. Hours of wading in shallow, boggy, grassy water will build strong legs and back. Continuous casting will build strong arms, especially when you're casting into a brisk wind. My right arm is three inches larger around than my left arm, mainly because I cast with it year round. On calm days I can cast—all day—up to 200 feet—150 into the wind. Plus, I think being around salt water is healthy for you.

Before I started wade fishing, I had normal colds and sinus problems. After I started, they disappeared. In fact, I haven't had any sinus problems or a serious cold in more than fifty years. I can get soaked and stay wet on cold winter days and never catch a cold. I've come to believe it's the salt water and my physical condition.

Once I slipped off a dock at 1 a.m. into thirty-nine degree water while carrying an outboard to put on my boat. I was fully clothed. Without changing clothes I climbed in my car and drove to an all-night store and bought two spark plugs for the motor, found an all-night laundromat, stripped, and put my clothes in a dryer. After they dried, I returned, put the spark plugs in the motor, cranked it, made a shell reef, and caught twenty trout before daylight. I never so much as got a sniffle. To this day I can still get soaked in salt water on cold days and never catch a cold. Yet if I get soaked in fresh water and have no dry change of clothes, I'll catch a cold every time.

There's also something about salt water that helps heal open wounds. One dark night in Offat's Bayou during the 1950s, a big trout slammed a treble hook into the back of my hand. I finally got the fish unhooked but the treble was embedded deep and I was hurting. So, I decided to yank the hook out, meat and all. It left a terrible looking hole. I got to my boat, warmed a pot of salt water, and submerged my hand in it for about forty-five minutes. By morning the soreness had gone from my hand, and I was able to keep fishing.

Salt water, like fresh water, contains bacteria and must be boiled before using it as a remedy. I recommend salt water to heal any open or fresh wound on the water, and wade fishing to help keep you strong and healthy throughout life.

These are just a couple of the many secrets of wade fishing I've set down in the pages that follow.

I hope you enjoy the book. And I hope you have great fishing!

Rudy Grigar—"The Plugger"

Contents

II

How to Wade Fish

Plugger

Introduction

"Rudy Grigar," outdoor writer Joe Doggett once wrote, "is part sea trout. He doesn't fish like a normal person because he studies fish in the bays like a person studies medicine—year round, day and night, regardless of the weather. He understands the movements of the tides and currents, the bait and the fish, and knows when and where they'll come together."

By most counts, Grigar is considered the best saltwater wade fisherman to ever wet a lure. He is an institution among wade fishermen—a lone wolf who, for more than half a century, has waded dark bays on moonless nights filling stringers; a master of the saltwater plug under any condition.

Grigar is the last of those who pioneered the sport and the light tackle that went with it. He was there when it started—developing, testing, experimenting with lures, rods, and line. He and a handful of others—the late Zollie Taliaferro, June Beckley, Elmer Hawkins, Marvin Burnett, Harry Reynolds, Phil Allen, Joe Riding, plug maker Doug English, "Pluggin' Shorty" (Anton Stettner) from Corpus Christi, and Houston's master rod maker Earl Lingo—pioneered Gulf Coast wade fishing and brought the sport into the twentieth century, before manufacturers took their ideas and designs and mass-produced them.

It could even be argued that Grigar, English, and Pluggin' Shorty helped start a lure industry for saltwater wade fishermen along the Gulf Coast. They developed, experimented with, then made hundreds of saltwater wood lures in home shops—now collector's items—before the days of mass lure production.

With the energy and enthusiasm of men half his age, Grigar has no intention of slowing down in his eighties. Perhaps it's because he has fed on the sand and salt of the Gulf where he has fished for almost six decades. He has probably pushed more water and caught more game fish on artificial lures—he hasn't used bait since 1924—than any other person alive. Grigar claims to have caught a million pounds of saltwater game fish. "If any man has," outdoor writer Bob Brister once wrote, "it's he."

Even among today's wade fishing "experts"—so called for commercial reasons—Grigar is the acknowledged authority on how to use the wade fisherman's rod, the saltwater lure, and the levelwind reel. His right arm is three inches larger around than his left—a casting oak rippled by veins. Unlike others who've spent their lives earning a living at something else, then writing about wade fishing, Grigar has spent his lifetime wade fishing and guiding wade fishermen in Gulf waters. He has had his pants ripped off at night in a chest-deep Galveston Bay by a shark hitting a full stringer tied to his belt; and has left full stringers as sharks larger than he approached his fish in daylight.

Undaunted, he fishes like there's no tomorrow and still eats everything he keeps. He feeds the fishermen he guides the fish they catch. At the end of this book, Grigar shares his basic recipes for saltwater game fish.

With the dramatic decline of the redfish population during the 1970s, Grigar and a few other sport fishermen—along with outdoor writers Bob Brister and Joe Doggett—helped form the Gulf Coast Conservation Association (GCCA). In return, he had his fishing camp destroyed on Panther Point and his life threatened. But the GCCA prevailed before commercial netters decimated the redfish.

Another Grigar trademark is that he stays about five years ahead of heavy fishing pressure. When he abruptly left the Texas coast during the late 1960s for the Chandeleur Islands—located about forty miles southeast of Louisiana's delta country, and south of Gulfport and Biloxi out in the Gulf—it wasn't, as Doggett wrote, ". . . to hunt sea shells."

Uncrowded and uninhabited, the Chandeleurs appealed to Grigar. Hurricanes routinely swept the islands clean of humans and structures. Miles of knee-deep fishing flats with clear, firm sandy bottoms—easy walking for an experienced wade fisherman stalking schools of speckled trout and redfish—stretched along the backside of the islands.

Grigar saw the islands as a final outpost, unspoiled, a last great fishing spot for a wade fisherman along the upper Gulf. He knew he'd found the place he would probably spend the rest of his life fishing, if a hurricane or shark didn't get him first.

Grigar set up camp—a small tent to keep the rain off—on the shore of Curlew Island. When the fishermen he'd guided before found out where he was, they flew in to fish with him. He lived off guide money, a few supplies, and the fish he caught.

As time passed, he built a small driftwood shack on the island. Then he spotted three fairly level sand dunes—two over water and one about 160 yards out from his shack. On each of the dunes he stuck a cane pole with a makeshift pin flag, and christened this his Par Three Chandeleur Country Club Golf Course. A pro golfer who fished with him sent him a tow-sack full of shag balls each year. When he was waiting for tides and good fishing, he would take an old golf club and shoot shag balls at the flags. He wasn't sure whether or not fish ate his slices.

In 1979, Hurricane Frederick blew his shack and the three-hole golf course away and put most of Curlew Island under water.

Determined not to let something like a hurricane get in the way of good fishing, Grigar made his way to Slidell, Louisiana, bought a new thirty-two foot houseboat that slept four and a new outboard, then navigated 125 miles through Louisiana's swamps and wetlands to the Chandeleurs.

A jetstream storm with hurricane-force winds sank the houseboat a couple winters later.

Most men sixty-four-years-old would have been devastated. Undaunted, Grigar traveled to Biloxi, Mississippi, this time purchasing a used, seaworthy, fifty-six foot, steel-hulled boat that slept nine with unheard of amenities such as air-conditioning, hot showers, and TV. And he bought a new twenty-one foot Boston Whaler to get across Chandeleur Sound in eight- to ten-foot seas, along with two aluminum skiffs, with 25-horse-power motors to shuttle fishermen to his honey holes.

Grigar returned to the Chandeleurs, this time anchoring behind North Island midway along the Chandeleur chain; ducking and running inland ahead of the hurricanes.

There are those who would raise an eyebrow towards anyone choosing to spend the greater portion of his time near a group of desolate, hurricane-swept islands. "Far removed," as Doggett wrote, "from the salvation of corner convenience stores. In less-than-insulated environments, things can go wrong—mosquitoes and jelly fish, sharks, and stingrays." (Grigar has been hit twice by stingrays.)

"Still," Doggett wrote, "there's a certain satisfaction of moving and casting, feeling the summer sun coming down, and the tug of a weighty surf stringer. It's a loose, laid-back feeling you don't get . . . in a supermarket."

During one of his last trips to the Chandeleurs, Doggett watched Grigar lecture other fishermen about the trip—master plugger and promoter—sharing several decades of successful wade fishing knowledge.

"That night," Doggett wrote, "Grigar spoke with uncharacteristic quietness. 'I'm running out of places,' he confided. 'When they take over the Chandeleurs, I'm running out of places. What worries me more is that maybe I'm starting to run out of time.'"

Fortunately, the Chandeleurs and the adjacent Delta wetlands have been designated National Wildlife Refuges, complete with their own game wardens. Structures, camping, and hunting on the islands are prohibited, but it's okay to fish them. The pristine chain will be spared mankind's technological miracles as we close out the twentieth century.

And Grigar? Well, he's semi-retired now and living in the country down near the tiny town of Pettus in South Texas; laying shag balls alongside makeshift golf pins about seventy-five yards out from his front door, and beating men two decades his junior in local golf tournaments.

Still, the Gulf pulls at him, drawing him back from time to time. And if you happen to hit the Laguna or the Chandeleurs at the right time of year, you might just run into him down there somewhere, wading grass flats and the edges of drop-offs, catching and cooking fish in the evenings, listening to the surf and the gulls, guiding a couple friends to guts and holes and reefs only he knows about—places where time brings the tides, fish, and a master saltwater plugger together.

W. R. McAfee

I
A History of Gulf Coast Wade Fishing

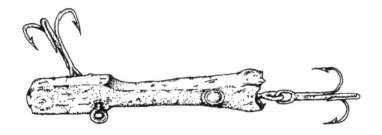

The Plugger comes by it naturally. When Rudy Grigar was born on April 29, 1915, his father, John J. Grigar was away fishing and duck hunting. In this photo, taken May Day 1915, John Grigar (right) has just returned from that trip with his nephew and arch sporting rival Alfred Grigar (left) and a friend, to discover he has a three-day old son. The Plugger says of his father and cousin, "they were the two Jungle Jims of the era, both big strong men, like two gorillas, wild horse bronco busters, both crack shots with any kind of a gun." Rudy and Alfred's son Erwin, carry on the family tradition, as the closest of friends and the staunchest of plug fishing rivals.

1

The Education of a Plug Fisherman

I was born in a farmhouse southwest of Houston near Wallis, Texas, and the San Bernard River on April 29, 1915. I had two older sisters—both of whom, like me, were delivered by my grandmother. She told me later I was three days old before my father ever saw me. He'd been hunting and arrived home with his old gray mare pulling his buggy. He had four large catfish and seventy greenhead mallards in back of the buggy. He'd only spent four twelve-gauge black powder shells to down the ducks.

Ducks and geese were literally wing to wing on ponds, lakes, and rice fields then. Those were days before rice tractors and combines. Rice was cut and bundled in small stacks by hand, and there was always lots left in the fields for ducks and geese which numbered in the tens of thousands.

Shotgun shells were a nickel apiece—a good sum to a family like ours. To save money and shells, hunters crawled to the edge of a pond or rice field, stood up, pulled the trigger twice, and picked up all the ducks or geese they could carry. The practice had been going on as long as they'd been manufacturing shotgun shells and continued on into the Depression years. In reality, this practice was the beginning of the end of an abundant duck population. They were slaughtered without concern or thought.

My first years and earliest recollection of fishing for something began beside a bullfrog pond behind the farmhouse where

I caught crawfish with twine and a piece of salt pork. When I was about four years old, I put a worm on a hook and caught my first mud cat. Catching that fish was about the best feeling a boy my age could have experienced back then. My mother cooked it for me. Four years later we moved to another farm close to the Brazos River. The Brazos was a much better fishing stream with a strong, deep current. My dad knew the dangers of the current and made all of us learn to swim. My first lesson was simple. He grabbed me, threw me in deep water, and watched me struggle. He was ready to rescue me if he had to, but I only required a couple of "lessons" and I began coming out on my own. The following summer I was playing alligator in the Brazos, which in some places was about two hundred yards wide and thirty feet deep. Alligator meant jumping off a high Brazos bank, submerging, and not showing your head until you reached the other side. If you came up for air before you got there, you lost the match. The spot where we jumped was only about eighty yards wide, but the river was deep and swift.

This was a golden era when the only pollution in the river came from cattle that decided to wade in and drink the clean water. It was a time when groups of deadhead country boys— usually about fifteen to twenty—got together on Sunday to swim nude and play alligator, which was about the only sport in those days besides scrub baseball and wrestling matches.

My dad raised corn, cotton, hay, and cattle. Our small farm was located just across the county line from the John Moore ranch, where my dad sometimes worked for extra money.

The ranch contained several thousand acres, stretched from Orchard to Rosenberg, Texas, and had only one cross fence that I can recall.

There were swamps all over the ranch, one of which held the prettiest, ten-acre natural bass lake you ever laid eyes on.

The fish in the lake were big and strong, and it was a natural, year-round habitat and nesting area for duck and other water critters.

All that changed in 1924, though. The first oil well—a gusher—was brought in near the lake. The owner gave everyone associated with the well and its drilling a new auto—a novelty at the time—then promptly drained the lake so they could drill more oil wells.

People came and gathered fish off the lake bottom. Many were used for fertilizer.

My dad also had a large cornfield alongside the Brazos River. The east side of the field was an old riverbed formed hundreds of years ago when the Brazos changed course. When the river flooded, it left a mile-long lake in the old channel. The lake was overgrown with yaupon on both ends and was a haven for bass, perch, and other game fish.

It was on this lake I first met August "Gus" Rohan in 1923. I was eight and he was an old immigrant who, I discovered, was an expert fisherman with a fly rod and homemade flies. In fact, he was catching bass—large bass—on hand-tied flies the first time I saw him.

Sometimes if Gus was fishing near where we were swimming, I'd get tired, dress, and go sit quietly on the bank and watch him catch fish. Occasionally a bullfrog would hit his fly. One day I asked him if he would show me how he did it. He agreed. Gus taught me more about fishing than any person before or since. I'll never forget the first thing he told me. He said, "Rudy, the most important thing about catching fish is to sneak up on them like you're stalking a deer or a pond full of mallards. Work very, very quiet and preferably alone. Fish are like any other wild animal. They're not dumb, and they spook easily."

To this day when I see a fisherman roar up to some hole or into a school of redfish then sit there for an hour and not catch anything, I still recall Gus's advice.

I began doing anything to earn a little money, saving my pennies until I had enough to get the catalog out and order me a small casting rig. Then I started to catch fish with Gus's lures. I was hooked.

Fish were plentiful in those days, but no one used lures to catch them. Everyone used the pole, line, hook, sinker, and seines. Mostly seines. People netted carp, buffalo, catfish, gar, and gaspergou by the wagonload with fifty-foot seines. Bass would usually jump the nets, but they'd seine enough to feed twenty-five to thirty people at the Sunday fish fry.

People socialized at these fish fries. There was plenty of fried fish, corn on the cob, bread, watermelon, and usually a tub of homemade beer or wine for the grown-ups. The youngsters would get up a scrub baseball game or the boys would wrestle.

All the while Gus continued to show me the tricks to fly-fishing and how to make my own flies. Gradually, I began to make my own lures. I started out carving them from bottle stopper corks, covering them with genuine frogskin, then painting them different colors and putting a hook on them. They worked, and I stopped using bait in 1924.

Understand, this was a time when you fished for bass in natural bodies of water like ponds, creeks, lakes, rice canals, and a few reservoirs. There weren't any man-made dams to speak of. The Brazos had a few natural lakes along the bottom that were good fishing, and there were Manor and Eagle Nest Lakes in West Columbia and Alcorn Lake in Sugarland, which was a good enough bass lake to require a full-time warden. There were a lake or two around Rosharon, as well.

Unfortunately all these lakes were private and could be fished by invitation only. They were well managed and stocked, however, and were always closed during the March-to-May spawn. People who saw the spawn said the fish were so thick they rubbed scales. Regardless, I can't remember a time when I couldn't catch twenty or thirty bass from these lakes in a couple of hours or less with my homemade lures. Grown men would stare at me.

I believe learning how to catch bass on artificial lures made me a better saltwater lure fisherman even though it isn't necessary for anyone wanting to take up saltwater plugging today.

In general, a bass is harder to catch than saltwater fish because he only feeds when his belly is empty or when he's perturbed at your lure for invading his turf. Saltwater game fish, on the other hand, are gluttons and never stop eating.

By 1925 I'd developed a reputation for catching fish on homemade plugs. My friends started calling me "Plugger," and the handle stuck. In fact, I was the only fisherman around then—besides Gus—who didn't use bait.

I decided early on if I was going to fish, I had to have a boat. I set about building my first one—a sixteen-footer—from scratch during the late 1920s. My high school manual class—shop classes they call them today—was in woodworking. Our teacher, Walter Wasicek, was an expert wood finisher and taught us to build stools, chairs, and tables that looked factory made. I sometimes helped my father carpenter, so I'd already become a pretty fair hand with wood. Everyone had to pick a project. I'd already decided on my boat.

I built it out of one-by-twelve, sixteen-foot planks—even the flat bottom and seats. I also added a one-by-four to the sides, which made it look much bigger and more seaworthy. I painted it green and white and christened it over the water. Outboards didn't exist then and for the next twenty years, my sixteen-footer was considered a large boat on freshwater lakes. It was watertight and I caught lots of fish out of it in deep water.

When the Depression hit, what little progress the tackle industry was making came to a standstill. Times were bad. No one had any money for anything, but we had plenty of fish and wild game. I spent those days fishing, hunting, playing a trumpet in a small jazz band, and working odd jobs.

I saved my money and moved to Houston in 1938. I think the population was about 80,000. I felt like a foreigner. Everyone there was well-groomed and dressed and seemed to have some money. My net worth was $1,200. Nonetheless, I found a good-looking used Ford pickup at "Sam the Rocket Man's" lot on Harrisburg Boulevard. Sam guaranteed the pickup had a good engine and four new tires. I plunked down $250 cash. For the

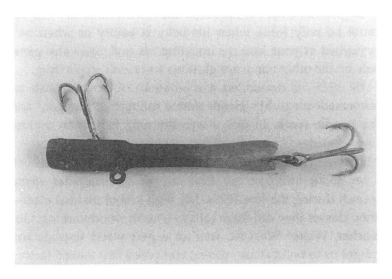

The original Plugger Toothbrush Lure, now a collector's item, was made from a toothbrush handle. The nose was weighted. The lure resembled a shrimp to the Gulf's game fish and was effective.

first time in my life, I had reliable fishing transportation when I could afford the gas.

Gradually I left the inland lakes and ponds and worked my way to the Gulf. I found saltwater fish hit lures hard and fought even harder. They were bigger, stronger, and better eating than freshwater fish, especially the redfish.

My first serious fishing expedition in the Gulf began as a duck hunt south of Rockport, Texas, in 1938. Opening day was bright sunshine and seventy degrees. The ducks were plentiful; but because of the clear weather, we couldn't get close to them. So, everyone decided to go saltwater fishing.

Being the youngest in the group, I was told to drive to Port Aransas and buy some live shrimp. Since I hadn't baited a hook since I was ten, I refused to use the shrimp. I always carried my fishing equipment in my pickup and had two Johnson Silver Spoons in my tackle box. I tied one on and pulled in more than sixty big speckled trout and redfish. The others couldn't believe it. In fact, hardly anyone believed speckled trout and redfish could be caught on anything other than live bait.

We were fishing an area called Estes Flats. It was located near Jimmy's Duck Hunting Lodge across Highway 35 from the carbon black plant in Rockport, Texas. The area became one of my honey holes. In fact, the hardware fishermen kept room No. 5 rented year round at the El Camino Courts which had just opened. We'd get there, check in, drive out to the flats, and wade into waist-deep water and fish. The only big hole in the entire bay was California Hole which was deep and boggy. Bait fishermen never bothered us, and we had the bay to ourselves. Buzz Hopkins and I caught thousands of large trout and redfish from these flats during the late 1930s—all on the Johnson Silver Spoon.

I found out later there were two fishermen in Corpus Christi who were using artificial lures during this era, as well. One was a fellow known as "Pluggin' Shorty" (Anton Stettner), and the other was a gentleman named Doug English. English eventually founded the Bingo Lure Company in Corpus Christi and was the first to mass-produce one of my lures—the "Plugger Bubble"—which virtually all of the early saltwater lure fishermen used. The company sold thousands of them. After Bingo went out of business, the Rudy's Bubble became a collector's item.

I developed another good saltwater lure that I whittled out of old amber toothbrushes. I would weight the curved nose of the brush, attach two treble hooks behind, and catch redfish and specks until I couldn't lift my stringer. To this day it's still an excellent lure.

I discovered there weren't many lures available for saltwater wade fishing. About the only good lures we had then were the Johnson Spoons, the Tony Acetta Spoon, Florida Shiners, and River Runts. Since no lures were being made along the Texas Coast for smaller (twenty pounds or less) saltwater game fish, I got busy in my woodshop and made hundreds from mahogany, then painted them different colors. Coloring those lures was another first. English and Shorty were doing the same. In

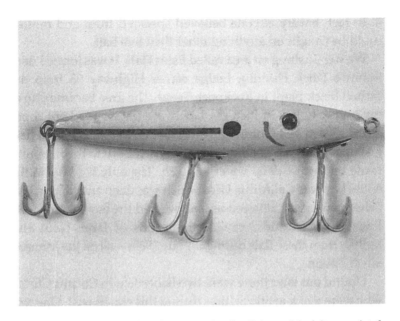

Original Mahogany Wade Fishing Lure. Another Grigar original, it was painted with seven coats of pearl nail polish and had an eye on the nose, which later became a standard. The position of the eye enabled casting into the wind and controlling depth by the speed of the retrieve.

my opinion we helped kick off a new era for the saltwater lure industry and wade fishing, in general. I remember Doug giving me a lure one day with one side painted red and the other side white. He said, "Plugger, take this lure and try it. Then give me a report which side they hit best." I also altered existing lures. I made floaters out of sinkers and vice versa, and I changed the eye from the top of my wade fishing lures to the nose—an original change which lure manufacturers picked up.

I always enjoyed catching fish with lures I made and passed out hundreds to my friends. Many times someone would knock at my door and say, "You promised me one of your lures. Sorry to wake you up in the middle of the night."

They're collector's items now, too.

2

When the Bays Were Filled with Redfish

Wade-fishing tackle and fishing equipment, in general, still weren't making much progress in the late 1930s. In 1939, there were only eight outboard motors over 33-horsepower registered in Houston. Four of these were owned by wade fishermen— "Captain" June Beckley, Zollie Taliaferro, Eddie Minor, and myself.

World War II interrupted everything and delayed both the production of outboard motors and fishing tackle. After the war, the government flooded the market with large, surplus outboards and landing boats—all reasonably priced and ideal for the sport fisherman.

Manufacturers switched from wartime production to commercial production and began putting new boats, outboards, and tackle on the market. Thousands of Texas fishermen, home from the war, began hitting the speckled trout and redfish along the Gulf on weekends, filling freezers, and for the first time putting pressure on the fish.

It was during this same period that Houston newspapers hung the title "hardware fishermen" on the few of us who used lures in salt water. Everyone else used live or cut bait, and saltwater lure fishermen were rare.

Our original group consisted of Taliaferro, Beckley, Earl Lingo (a master rod maker who made all my rods until his death in 1990), Elmer Hawkins, Eddie Oliver (a Texas Ranger captain),

Plugger found these bays filled with redfish and speckled trout in the early days, before World War II and pollution.

and Minor (who developed perforator guns for the oil fields), and myself.

Oliver's and Minor's jobs kept them on the road a lot, but they were still considered a part of the original group. Together we fished West and East Galveston Bays and kept a wade-fishing secret under wraps until Houston's outdoor writers put the word out.

Our secret? Night fishing.

I discovered night fishing by accident on September 1, 1946—Labor Day weekend. We'd heard the surf along Galveston Island and Freeport was clear all the way to the beach, with specks wall to wall.

At the time there was no connection or bridge over San Luis Pass then. We flipped a coin to decide which side to fish. The Freeport side won. We set up camp on Saturday afternoon and caught trout all evening on silver spoons with white bucktails. These were the days before gold and copper spoons, which were introduced during the 1950s. After a meal of fresh-fried specks, everyone except me went to sleep. About midnight I picked up my rod and walked to the beach. It was a moonless night and completely dark. You had to watch for rattlesnakes around San Luis Pass then, and I've often found them in the surf—I guess waiting for a fish to come close enough to bite.

What I found that night in the surf, though, were Spanish mackerel so thick you couldn't stir them with a stick—all nice, big, line peelers. I shook everyone awake, and the five of us caught and released at least two hundred mackerel. Occasionally we'd land a big speck, but the mackerel were so thick the trout had little chance to hit the spoons.

This action continued until daylight when the fish suddenly stopped feeding—just like that. You couldn't have seined one out of the surf which, a few minutes before, had been churning with them.

The morning broke perfect with just a ripple on the beach. Carloads of day fishermen began arriving with their live shrimp and popper corks. We decided to stay and see if anyone caught

Catches such as these were common along the Gulf Coast during the first part of the century. These specks and reds were taken at night in East Galveston Bay. The "convertible" top on the boat was an early adaptation for wade fishing during the Gulf's winter months. Elmer Hawkins, left, is one of the original group of saltwater lure fishermen.

Catch from East Galveston Bay, circa early 1950s. Fish were taken on the Johnson Sprite Spoon.

A thirty-five pound red bull taken from and released in West Galveston Bay, circa late 1940s.

anything on the live bait. We didn't see a single fish landed. We knew, then, nights were when the really good fishing action was. We began to plan our regular fishing trips accordingly.

During the summer months, we would make a freezer of ice cream and rest during the day while everyone ran around the bay boating and fishing. On weekends the bays were especially crowded with daytime boat traffic, which kept both bait and game fish disturbed. By sunset the boats would all have headed home and the fish would be hungry. After the boaters left, we would hit our spots in the bay. Sometime after dark the fish

Catches off Hanna's Reef, circa late 1949, early 1950.

Stringer of speckled trout and redfish taken at night off Hanna's Reef, 1954.

would start feeding. When they did, you couldn't reel them in fast enough.

Wade fishing in total darkness is exciting. You cast your lure into the dark, hear a loud splash as a red hits it, and feel your rod bend double. Although night fishing for bass was popular prior to this—especially with noisy top-water lures like Jitterbugs, crippled minnows, and plunkers—few people thought about wade fishing for speckled trout or reds at night with lures. Besides there being very few saltwater fishermen who knew how to plug then, a dark bay can be a menacing place, with sharks and stingrays and all. Everyone just fished during the day with live or cut bait.

We kept night fishing and the techniques we developed to go with it a secret for several years. Then the outdoor writers for the Houston newspapers heard about us and started following our nighttime excursions.

Houston had three major newspapers at the time—the *Houston Chronicle*, the *Post*, and the *Press*. Fishing news in all of them was pretty much the same: live bait scarce, fishing slow, and reports from bait camps of a few redfish being taken in the grasses along West Bay on live shrimp and cut mullet. If you read the Monday report, you had your fishing news for the rest of the week. Only the tide's schedule and weather report changed. The *Post's* Bill Walker was knocking on Taliaferro's door on Telephone Road at least once a week, wanting to know what kind of action the "hardware" fishermen were into. During this same period, the *Press* folded.

Bob Brister realized the need for a different approach to fishing news when he became editor of the *Chronicle's* fishing section in the late 1940s. He was a good East Texas bass fisherman and a good shot with a shotgun but at the time had very little firsthand knowledge about saltwater lure fishing. Brister was curious about the emerging sport and began to go with us on our fishing runs. He became a good wade fisherman, photographed the action as he went, and began to write about saltwater lure fishing. Later, Joe Doggett joined the *Chronicle* staff, became a good wade fisherman as well, and continued writing about lures and saltwater wade fishing. Brister and Doggett were instrumental in introducing the sport of wade fishing to the public. Both became nationally known outdoor writers, as well.

Then Harv Boughton and Stan Slaten—both with the *Post*, and both with lure fishing experience—began writing about wade fishing. Slaten and Boughton also went on to become nationally known outdoor writers. Shortly afterward, the *New Orleans Times Picayune* and the Biloxi, Mississippi *Herald* picked

In his entire career, Plugger landed only three over-ten-pound speckled trout. This, the last one, was taken in West Bay near San Luis Pass, November 1956.

up on the emerging sport and the outdoor equipment manufacturers began zeroing in on the lure and tackle markets that went with it. The sport really turned the corner during the 1950s when Slaten began to host a television fishing show. Several other pros and I made appearances—for the first time—on Channel 39 in Houston. After that, our nighttime secret was out, and wade fishing was on its way. The articles written by this handful of outdoor writers during the 1940s, 1950s, and 1960s—coupled with Slaten's television show—triggered the popularity of wade fishing as a sport.

West Galveston Bay was still primitive after World War II. There were no developments, and Earl Galceran was about the only fisherman other than commercial netters living on the south shore of West Bay. There were places there even I hadn't fished. The whole shoreline from Starvation Cove to San Luis Pass was just like the Indians left it.

During World War II, San Luis Pass, parts of West Galveston Bay, and all of Christmas Bay were closed to fishing traffic.

These areas were used for practice bombing runs with live ammunition. They were bombed over and over throughout the war, leaving hundreds of deep potholes—many ten to fifteen feet deep.

Speckled trout and redfish were wall to wall in these holes after the war, and we treated this bit of knowledge like a military secret. The large grass flat just east of Bird Island near San Luis Pass had hundreds of potholes. On warm days when the water came in clear through the pass, speckled trout and redfish would drop down in these cool holes by the hundreds. We would wade fish near these deep holes, cast over them, and bring our lures across the top. We'd have a speck or red on every cast. This action lasted three or four years until hurricanes and storm currents sanded in the holes. Then, construction began on a bridge and road to connect Galveston and Freeport. This road and the bridge over San Luis Pass were the beginning of the end of the great fishing in the pass.

Fascinating to me in the early days were the schools of trout and redfish. Being able to fish at least three nights a week, I had the bay "wired" and was able to stay on top of the fish as they moved. There were no limits then on any fish.

Huge schools of redfish—sometimes up to five hundred—would move together in the bays. I noticed these schools were always comprised of the same size fish. Some schools would be in the seven-pound class, others in the ten-pound class, but always of equal size.

I concluded the schools were from the same hatch and stayed together for long periods of time, perhaps their entire lives. This schooling phenomenon occurred around September 1 and lasted into winter. During the winter months I stayed with the schools, learning how and when they would move over certain areas. I required very little sleep and could fish twenty-four hours without getting tired.

I liked night fishing best. No lights. The darker the better. On clear, calm nights, I could see from the reflection of stars off the

Checking a nice stringer with Lee Brinton, left, taken in West Galveston Bay, June 17, 1958.

water once my eyes got used to the dark. I could even change reels and tie lures by starlight.

To locate fish on these nights, I listened. When a large school of redfish moved, a large school of baitfish always moved ahead of them. Both schools sounded like freight trains churning through the darkness. The closer they got, the louder the noise. I'd have my boat anchored where I could drop into the water and move to a point where I could cast into the baitfish. If I was fast, I'd land two or three ten-pounders before they rushed past.

Sometimes the school would move right through me, bumping my legs or chest. Then, they would be gone. Soon, another school would pass; and I'd repeat the process until I had a full stringer.

San Luis Pass was a great place to fish lures then. A few surf fishermen using cut bait would show up on weekends, but most of the time the beach was deserted and undeveloped. You could

*Stringer of reds taken off
Bird Island, August 15, 1958.*

drive to the pass at low tide from either side but it took a couple hours of fighting logs and deep sand and waiting for low tide to drive back.

Peterson's Fishing Camp in Chocolate Bayou was one of our landing places and was the best way to get to the pass. We would set up tents at the pass and work the bay, wade fishing for reds and speckled trout. We had good access to Christmas Bay, Bastrop Bay, and Bird Island. All these places were still undeveloped, unpolluted, and full of fish during the 1940s.

For twenty-five years Bird Island was a tremendous spot for lure fishing, the best in Galveston Bay. The island was located just inside the north side of San Luis Pass and had a very deep channel along the west end. The drop-off was sharp, about fourteen feet straight down, and currents through the channel were strong. The east side of Bird Island had a deep drop-off and channel, as well.

Along the north end of Bird Island were large, shallow, grassy flats. The flats covered about forty acres and were ideal fishing if you knew how to fish the tide coming through the pass.

When the tide rose, you caught fish on the east side. When it turned back, you caught fish on the west side and on the shallow north end. At night fish would cover the north flat when the tide ran out. We would always be there late in the evening, about dark, after the day fishermen had left. Trout, redfish, mackerel—everything would be there feeding. On several occasions, I witnessed the entire flats—all forty acres or so—covered with feeding fish.

The water covering these grassy flats would be less than two feet deep. We would wade within casting distance of the drop-offs, kneel down, and cast just over the edge where the fish were following the tide, feeding. By doing this, we avoided strong tide currents in the channel and the large sharks that followed the fish. The fish liked to work the shallow water close to the drop-off.

Lure fishermen kept a tight lip about spots like the Bird Island flats. The secret was to be there late in the evening after all the other boats had gone and things returned to normal. The flats were ideal for a Johnson Silver Spoon with a single hook, and fish were easy to land. Since we were kneeling, we simply held our fish down, unhooked them, and either strung them or released them if they were small.

Our group of saltwater pluggers caught tons of fish on Bird Island for more than twenty-five years. Before Beckley died at age 92, he and I calculated we spent almost a thousand nights fishing there together, always with artificial lures; and this was just one spot. East Galveston Bay and the Port O'Connor land cut were two other spots we fished regularly.

Another fishing friend, Bill Wortham, and I planned a trip to West Bay in 1949. His boat was moored at La Porte, Texas. The trip was scheduled for at least four days and nights. The weather looked good, and we had plenty of food and ice chests for our fish. We got a late start and made Texas City by sundown. Since we'd planned for four days, we were in no hurry to get to West Bay. We decided to spend the first night in East Galveston Bay near Smith's Point. The weather was calm. Early the next morning I noticed a bunch of water turkeys sitting on an exposed shell reef. We checked our charts and found we were about a quarter mile from Hanna's Reef. There was a light fog and fish slicks around the island. The area just "looked" fishy. We decided to try the place and hit West Bay the next day.

I made coffee while Bill backed the boat against the reef and anchored. We pulled on our waders, dropped into the water, and immediately began catching five- to seven-pound trout. The bottom was hard and easy wading, and trout were wall to wall.

From that day Hanna's Reef became another favorite spot of ours. Today it still produces good fish and is one of the best night fishing spots in the Gulf. Bill and I never made it to West Bay because we suddenly found our ice chests full of fish. We decided to unload and nearly didn't make it home. When we tried to start the motor, we found the battery was dead. Then, we twisted off the hand crank trying to start it.

We didn't see another boat the whole day. Understand, this was 1949. We weren't worried, though, because we had plenty of food and water. We decided the only thing left to do was rig a sail with bed sheets and set out, which we did that night and most of the next day without seeing another boat. Finally we got within sight of the ship channel—about a mile away—and saw a boat passing. We waved a black coat, but the boat continued on. Just as it was about to disappear, it turned around and came back. Someone had seen us. It turned out to be a Brown and Root construction crew boat from the same marina. They gave us a battery, and we made it to port.

The west end of Hanna's Reef is about a quarter mile long and is exposed at all times. When the tide is moving strong—in or out—fish pass the ends of the reef going around it. The best

These big redfish were taken Thanksgiving eve off Hanna's Reef on three-quarter-ounce Johnson Sprite Spoons with orange bucktails. Allen H. Russell, left, was president of the old Houston Buffs baseball team. Circa early 1950s.

action is always around the west end with the incoming tide. When the tide runs out, the action shifts to the east side.

For more than three decades, Beckley and I caught thousands of trout and redfish around the ends of Hanna's Reef at night. We would always wade out and see if they were feeding, checking every thirty minutes or so. They might not be there right at first, but sometime during the night when the tide was running, the fishing action would turn on fast and furious. When it did, we caught big fish until our wrists ached.

The best time to fish Hanna's Reef is during the fall—October, November, and December. The best lure to use at the reef is a three-quarter-ounce Johnson Sprite Spoon, silver with a white bucktail and a single hook. The single hook is safer to handle in the dark and is easier to unhook from your fish. Multihooks always wind up injuring your fish.

One night Beckley and I were camped on the shoreline opposite Hanna's Reef. We fixed a good meal of fresh-shucked oysters we'd picked up off the reef that evening. The weather was absolutely perfect, about forty degrees with a cloudy drizzle overhead that kept starlight off the water. There was a light northeast wind and fog on the water. Best of all, it was dark as a grave.

About 10 p.m. I waded to the east end of the reef, positioned myself in waist-deep water, dropped my lure on top of the backbone, and let it float out with the tide into the drop-off beyond. The redfish were at the drop-off feeding—a large school of ten- to twelve-pounders. The action was hectic. I had twenty-six big, heavy redfish on my stringer within an hour. I was catching reds so fast—and because it was so dark—I held my stringer between my teeth while I reeled the next red in. There wasn't time to tie and untie to my waist.

The last red I landed was a big, heavy fish over twelve pounds. I stuffed him on my stringer and bit down on the rope again, but the red had no intention of staying on the stringer. He shot back down the stringer and popped the rope out of my mouth and three of my front teeth along with it. I spit the teeth

"Captain" June Beckley, one of the original saltwater lure fishermen, displays catch taken off Hanna's Reef, December 2, 1958. By their mutual estimation, Plugger and Beckley spent around a thousand days and nights fishing together.

These twenty-seven redfish were caught on a foggy night in West Galveston Bay on No. 3 Johnson Sprite Spoons, November 21, 1959.

out and grabbed hold of my stringer before it drifted to deep drop-off water and the sharks. Then I landed number twenty-seven. I'm still using the same bridge that replaced those teeth!

About 1 a.m. one morning during the late 1940s, I motored across West Galveston Bay to flounder the north shore. The weather was nice, and the wind was calm. I crossed the bay with my compass on a southeast reading, grounded my boat somewhere along the south shoreline, and went to sleep.

At daylight I saw I'd landed on the grassy point where Jamaica Beach Development sits today. The area then was completely undeveloped. I made myself a cup of coffee and sat on my large Monel ice chest looking at the sunrise, a calm Gulf, and a peaceful morning, enjoying the fact I was alive.

About a mile from me, someone started a loud outboard—about 10 or 12 horsepower—on a small aluminum boat. I can still hear its noise, even though it has been more than forty

Zollie Taliaferro, one of the original "hardware" (lure) fishermen, along the Gulf Coast, pulls a full stringer of specks and reds aboard after a successful afternoon of wade fishing. Circa late 1950s.

years. I remember the outboard because it stirred five huge schools of redfish, one right where I was anchored. Suddenly, for at least two hundred square feet around the boat, the water became a moving strawberry patch of reds. They'd been just beneath the surface feeding in the grassy flats around me. I'd been sitting right on top of them in my shorts, barefooted, sipping a cup of coffee. I noticed other large schools of reds about two hundred yards farther out in the flats. I sat my coffee cup down, dressed, slipped into my waders, and eased into the water in record time. My tackle was already rigged with a silver spoon.

The reds swam around me and between my legs. When I waded into deeper water, some hit me on the chin and chest. They were big, heavy fish, all about twelve pounds. I played with one of those fish a few minutes and only took two from the first school. By the time I landed the second one, the school had moved into deeper water. It didn't matter. I simply eased out to the other schools. They were smaller fish—five to seven pounds—and I managed about eight from each school.

Other good night fishing spots in West Galveston Bay then were South Deer Island and Long Reef. We had the wind and tide figured one night, knew which way the fish would be moving, and invited Brister from the *Chronicle* to join us.

Federal Reef, which is about a mile long with deep water on both sides, is probably still one of the most productive night spots around. You can either wade fish up and down the reef or, if you're a boat fisherman, anchor on either end in deep water and catch fish. On Long Reef, you stand just back of the reef, cast over it, and let your lure float into the deep drop-off. The east end is a natural. It drops off sharply—fourteen to twenty feet—while the reef itself is only two to four feet under water and is usually covered with oysters and baitfish all night.

Offat's Bayou remains another hot fishing hole on nights when northwest winds blow strong, cold fronts onto the bayou. This weather empties the warm water through south of Deer Island. When the weather turns cold, the fish work against the wind and drop into the deep blue hole in Offat's. After a warm-up, the fish come up and make their way back into the bay and feed until another cold front comes through. This pattern has held true for as long as I can remember.

3

The 1951 Fish Freeze

In 1951, a severe fish freeze occurred all along the Texas coast. There had been others—a major freeze in 1940 and a lesser one in 1947—but this one was by far the worst since World War II. This freeze was significant because the Gulf's game fish population suddenly found itself in trouble. In my opinion, the redfish and speckled trout populations along the Texas coast never recovered from the combined effects of the 1951 freeze and the steadily increasing postwar overfishing.

It's difficult for people to understand what a major freeze and fish kill is like unless they've seen one. When the freeze hit, I was in the water at Port O'Connor fishing Army Hole.

The next morning it was lined with dead fish. Curious, I hopped into my boat and ran the shoreline. What I saw was stunning. As far as you could see—I found out later, for hundreds of miles up and down the Texas and Louisiana coast—fish were stacked like cordwood on the shore. In some places the piles were twenty feet wide and three feet deep. They estimated that there were millions of pounds of dead fish all the way from Baffin Bay to the Sabine, even down to Eighth Pass in Mexico.

Pelicans and sea gulls were beginning to feed on the dead or sluggish fish, and the odor had already started. The water along the shoreline—clear and about three feet deep—was covered with dead fish.

This stringer of small specks was taken at San Luis Pass in 1953 after the major freeze in 1951 wiped out coastal fish as far as the Eighth Pass in Mexico. Plugger recalls no keeper trout until late 1951. Because pollution was not yet a problem, the fish population was already bouncing back.

Specks taken during the mid-1950s along Texas's Gulf Coast continued to increase in size after the hard coastal freeze of 1951. This stringer was taken near San Luis Pass.

Then I noticed a very curious thing. There weren't many dead redfish. I put two and two together and fished the deep west end of Army Hole from the bank that same afternoon and caught a stringer of redfish on a slow-moving lure across a twenty-foot bottom. They'd survived the freeze and were hungry.

The next day was very cold and still, but the sun was out. I waded slush ice along the shoreline and noticed mullet lying dormant on the bottom. When I poked them with a stick, they would come to life and swim away. A second major freeze occurred in 1983 all the way from Brownsville to Louisiana. I was fishing in the Chandeleur Islands off southern Louisiana when the freeze hit. Temperatures dropped below freezing for several days. Ice was ten inches thick over the flats and covered my private oyster beds for four days and nights. Yet my oysters revived; I don't think I lost one, and we didn't lose any fish in the Chandeleurs because they had access to deep water where they escaped the freeze. I found dormant mullet in about three feet of water; but when I poked them, they swam away.

These cold-weather kills are natural occurrences and have happened intermittently for thousands of years and will continue to happen for thousands of years unless man alters the weather. But freezes weren't responsible for the decline of the game fish.

The problem was the Gulf's shallows had never been fished like they were right after World War II. Up until then, the Gulf's game fish population had been able to regenerate itself naturally after a freeze. But combined with the overfishing, the freezes tilted the scales in the other direction. I saw smaller schools and fewer fish—in comparison to what I was used to seeing—for years after the 1951 freeze.

I also observed that specks cannot handle freezes as well as redfish. In fact, specks cannot survive a hard freeze in water shallower than eight feet. To survive a freeze, a speck needs at least twelve to sixteen feet of water where he'll submerge, become dormant, and lie on the bottom until the water warms.

Redfish, on the other hand, are much tougher and can survive the same freeze in shallow water. Not only will the red survive, he'll continue to feed throughout the freeze. Also, redfish can survive in abnormally warm water better than specks.

There are good conservation efforts underway today, but all the conservation efforts, legislation, strict limits, and controlled breeding programs should be considered at best only temporary relief.

Why? Because another hard freeze—which is sure to come— will again kill 80 percent of the fish in the Gulf's shallows; in particular, the Laguna Madre.

The alternative outlined below will give the Laguna's game fish a chance to escape the freeze.

- Open fish passes (land cuts) from the Laguna into the Gulf.
- Dredge channels (small ones that would serve as entrances) into deep holes in the Laguna—such as Army Hole at Port O'Connor.
- Ban all fishing along the coast during the freezes.

If left alone, most dormant fish in cold weather will recover if they have a hole or gulf to go to.

The only large, natural-breeding water along the Texas coast is the Laguna Madre. Fish come to it naturally to breed and to spawn.

To keep these fish from getting trapped in the Laguna, at least three—but ideally four or five—permanent fish passes cut to the Gulf are needed. These passes would connect the two bodies of water so the fish can escape a hard freeze as well as the hot—and just as lethal—water during summer heat surges and high salinity in the Laguna.

All the fish have now is an isolated hole or two and the Intracoastal Waterway, which runs the entire length of the Laguna. The canal would be an ideal place for fish during a freeze except that heavy barges passing through the canal churn it inside out.

When this happens, fish lying dormant in cold weather are churned up to shallow water or onto the shore where they freeze and die. If no passes are available to the fish, perhaps barge traffic in the canal could be halted for a day or two until the weather warms, giving the fish a chance to survive.

Until these priorities are set in motion and completed, all the conservation efforts in the world are at best only temporary, and will not save a single fish during the next hard freeze.

4

The Laguna Madre's Great Eighth Pass

Once I learned where the reefs and flats were in an area and how the fish moved, I was always ready to move on, always looking for new spots to wade and clear water—flats where the grass always seemed a little greener, the fish a little bigger. Matagorda Bay, San Antonio Bay, Aransas Bay, Corpus Christi Bay, Upper Laguna Madre, Baffin Bay, Lower Laguna Madre—I've waded them all. I made my first trip to Eighth Pass (now called Seventh Pass) in Mexico on the Lower Laguna Madre in 1946.

You couldn't drive to Eighth Pass then. You had to travel cross-country to Soto la Marina. It took sixteen to eighteen hours to get there, twenty-four if it was raining—if you could get there at all. Mostly, you traveled cross-country through brush and cow trails. From Soto la Marina you made your way east toward where La Pesca is today. Somewhere along the way you hired a Mexican skiff to take you the six miles across the Laguna Madre to Eighth Pass.

Once there, I would camp near the pass and wade fish the lagoon inside. What I found in that lagoon were twenty-pound snook and some of the greatest light tackle fishing I've ever experienced. There's nothing quite like hooking a twenty-pound snook on light tackle and spoon. He fights and jumps like a tarpon and goes airborne many times before you land him. Plus, he's one of the finest eating fish in the world. The tarpon has zero food value. I would fill a five-hundred-pound icebox with eighteen- to twenty-five-pound snook in forty-eight hours every time I made it to Eighth Pass. Everything else— redfish, trout, mackerel, flounder—I released. I caught hundreds of snook in that lagoon during the 1940s using Johnson Sprite Spoons with orange bucktails. Eighth Pass was then among the finest snook fishing spots in the world.

I always checked the prevailing winds before I made my Mexico runs. The reason being, as Zollie Taliaferro used to say, "A west wind will muddy up a fifty-foot well in Texas and Mexico."

It's true. When the wind turns from the west or southwest along the Texas coast, wade fishermen might as well pour water on the fire and head for the house unless they're in a protected cove or bay. West winds muddy coastal waters and keep tides low. To fish in the face of them generally is a waste of time.

This is especially true along the Mexican coast and the lower Laguna Madre. That's why I always checked weather reports before I made my trips to Mexico. Prevailing winds were my number one consideration in a go or no-go situation, hurricanes notwithstanding.

Once started, I always took enough food and gear for at least a week in case I had to wait out the wind or weather. August, September, and October—the hurricane months—were always the best fishing times. Of the forty or so trips I made to Eighth Pass during the 1940s and 1950s, I found the weather perfect for wade fishing no more than six times when I got there; and I would usually have to wait. But the wait was always worth it.

By the 1950s the lower passes had begun to sand up, and the tides couldn't get inside the Laguna Madre. Most of the inland water died or became too salty for fish until a hurricane would open the Laguna's passes and flush it out. I fished the Third, Fourth, Fifth, and Sixth Passes when I could, but none of these compared to the great snook fishing around Eighth Pass.

I stopped fishing the passes during the 1950s and didn't go back until 1972 when I got a call from a Dr. Estill, a good lure fisherman and friend, saying he wanted to put together a trip to Eighth Pass in October. I agreed to go with him.

We had a Blazer towing two Boston Whalers. Curtis Stockton, a golf pro, came along with us in his Oldsmobile, which turned out to be a real "mudder" when we hit rain-soaked dirt roads.

We spent the first night in Brownsville and reached San Fernando the next day, some eighty miles south, only to find the roads impassable due to heavy rains. We decided to push on south towards Soto la Marina and the new jetties, where we caught and cooked several redfish and flounder for supper.

The next day we returned to San Fernando, but the roads were still impassable. There was nothing to do but rent a couple rooms in San Fernando and wait for the weather to clear.

It didn't.

Finally we decided if we were going to fish that lagoon, our only alternative was to leave the boats in San Fernando and send everything else, us included, across fifty miles of mud on a Mexican grain truck.

We contracted with a driver to make the trip and settled on fifty dollars—half up front and half when he came back to pick us up a week later. He agreed. We loaded our gear onto the truck, crawled up on top of everything and started out. It took us all night—ten hours—to make the fifty miles to the lagoon. It was the roughest ride I ever made and over some of the worst roads I'd ever seen. No one rested or ate the whole trip.

We arrived at the shore the next morning at 9 a.m. but were still seven miles from the Eighth Pass by boat. About noon we located a Mexican fisherman with a rickety looking old boat, an old twenty-five-horsepower Johnson motor, and several skiffs. The motor had no observable cooling system and looked like a pile of junk, but it ran. We decided to take a chance.

We loaded five of the fisherman's skiffs to the gills and climbed into his boat. He started his funny-looking sea train towards the pass. The waters were rough and the going slow, but we got there around 9 p.m. We were wet, tired, hungry, and covered with mosquitoes. We set up camp around midnight

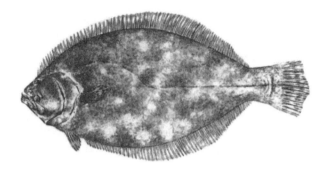

Typical Gulf flounder. Artwork courtesy Texas Parks and Wildlife Graphic Arts Department.

and wanted to fry a hot meal of fish. That's when we discovered our big bottle of cooking oil had broken sometime during the trip. So, we settled for a sandwich.

Without oil it would be impossible to fry fish, which we ate almost every meal when we fished, and there was a good possibility we might run short of food. So, we took a chance and sent our Mexican fisherman back for cooking oil. He returned the next day with our oil and two skiffs full of Federales following him. They were decked out in their finest regalia and machine guns, shook us down for another fifty dollars and our sipping whiskey, and left.

The good news was it didn't get any worse after that. In fact, their departure was the turning point of a memorable trip. The weather and water cleared the next day, and we found large "saddle blanket-sized" flounder so thick you almost stepped on them. We gigged a hundred the first two nights, put them on ice, and started eating them every meal. I landed one over-nine-pound flounder—the second largest in my lifetime—on a lure. I intended to have it mounted, but someone cut its head off and tossed it in the pot for supper before I had a chance to say anything.

Stockton caught and released more than a hundred speckled trout in one morning. The snook we caught were small and disappointing. We released most of them and switched to specks and reds. We caught everything near the Eighth Pass in the surf. The tide was low and we found the big fish just beyond in deep water. We filled our ice chests.

Tuesday came, and it was time to make our way back to shore with our catch and equipment. The truck was waiting to take us back, but the fee had doubled. We'd figured on that and had the ante waiting. Besides, we were already planning our next trip to Eighth Pass, this time without having to rely on the truck.

Up until then it was said a trip to Eighth Pass was impossible by vehicle. Estill didn't believe it. When he got back, he talked a Houston garage into rigging a special four-wheel-drive Blazer with a trailer hitch—both outfitted with large balloon tires—plus a cut-down Volkswagen with extra large twenty-two-inch balloon tires to crawl sand dunes and scout for the Blazer.

The Volkswagen would cut trail, and the Blazer would pull the equipment. All the tires could be deflated about 40 percent. We carried two automatic air pumps to fix flats, installed two heavy-duty winches to pull us out of mud and sand, and made plans for just about every contingency. Estill was determined to be the first vehicle expedition to make it to the lagoon in Eighth Pass.

Our fishing party consisted of seven lure fishermen, their equipment, supplies for a week, a thousand pounds of block ice, and a hundred pounds of dry ice for the fish. We tried to plan for everything—a good rule to always remember, even if you're only going for a short trip.

The weather was calm and clear all the way to the beach beyond Soto la Marina. At the beach we found waves were minimal with just a lap of water reaching the sand. From Soto to Eighth Pass is about sixty miles. It's extremely rough, and there's no exposed beach except at low tide. Otherwise, it's sand dunes and thornbushes all the way.

We began the trip early in the morning, five fishermen in the Blazer and two in the scout car. Those in the "bug" would work ahead four or five miles, then return and guide the Blazer and trailer. It was slowgoing, but it worked. We caught low tide in the lagoon and took advantage of the exposed, deserted beach, sometimes hitting fifty miles an hour for short runs. When the Blazer got stuck we'd roll out the two hundred feet of cable and winch it out. When we hit heavy dunes, we deflated the tires to about 40 percent and had very little problem. Twelve hours later, just before sundown, we made camp beside Eighth Pass in Mexico.

It was the last place in the world we expected to see other fishermen—but there they were, two of them . . . and from Houston. They couldn't believe we were just driving up to the pass. They'd reached the pass by floatplane. They said we might as well burn our vehicles as to try to make it back. They thought we'd just hopped in, got lucky, and drove down. We let on like we thought everyone drove to Eighth Pass.

We'd hoped to catch snook, but all we managed the first couple of days were specks, reds, and flounder. We also caught and released hundreds of blues, skipjack, ladyfish, and mackerel. I was fishing an area just off the old closed Eighth Pass where a small channel had pushed into the lagoon. Ten- to twelve-pound redfish in small schools were tailing in shallow waters within casting distance. Grass was even with the water, and you had to use a floating lure cast directly on top of the fish. I tied on a Rudy's Bubble.

The fish would surface for short periods. When they did, I put the bubble with a single hook and six-inch tailer—also with a single hook and white bucktail to hide the point—directly on top of them. They took it as quick as it hit the water, and I had one on every cast.

After four or five hours of this action, my fifteen-foot stringer was full. I started toward camp some five miles away, wading the surf with twenty-five ten- to twelve-pound reds floating behind me.

The next morning we hit the surf, which was fairly clear and in good shape. We landed several reds around ten pounds and about a hundred trout, cooked a good meal of fish, took a short siesta, and hit it again. The action remained the same—redfish and lots of trout in the pass.

The next morning I decided to make a special effort to locate some snook, which was the main reason I came. I worked my way three or four miles south down the beach, scouting. All I could find was eight- to ten-pound reds and schools of tarpon. I hooked and landed several twenty-pound tarpon and released them all.

After five miles I started back down the beach toward camp. It was around 10 a.m., and the tide had started out. I was in surf when I walked upon a school of large snook in front of me next to the bank. I froze, eased my lure right among them, and had a snook on every cast. They were all over ten pounds, a tremendous school of snook.

I waved at Charlie Fisher, a Pennzoil pilot who'd been raised in Jamaica. He'd grown up catching and eating snook. Like me, he had come for these fish. He was in the surf about a mile away and joined me. By the time we quit to return to camp, our stringers were so heavy with snook we could barely pull them through the surf.

When we got back, another group of official-looking Mexicans paid us a visit with machine guns, shook us down for a few dollars, and left.

The next day the pass was perfect. A Mexican boatman told me about a grassy flat he'd seen, and I talked him into taking Curtis and me there. He crossed the pass to a deep gut that spread into a large, grassy flat where it ended. He dropped us off and left.

We waded almost to the edge of the gut, cast out over it, and started catching fish every cast—snook, trout, and redfish. Between the two of us we had over a 100 solid fish in a couple of hours. At 11 a.m. my nineteen-foot stringer was so full I couldn't get another fish on it. There was nothing to do but wait for the boat.

When we got back to camp, we iced our fish, broke camp, and headed back. We had good weather and low tide all the way out. It was my last trip to Eighth Pass and will always be one of my fondest fishing memories.

5

Watching the Decline of Game Fish Along the Texas Coast

Port O'Connor, the land cut, and the Upper and Lower Laguna Madre were always my favorite wade fishing areas during the early years and were among the most popular fishing spots in Texas. I started wade fishing the Laguna during the 1930s, then the Port O'Connor area during the 1940s with Ed Payne and Louis Kasmoraski.

One fall trip with Bill Wortham stands out in my mind. He and I hitched my Helton Clinker and 33-horsepower Evinrude to his new 1949 Chevrolet and headed for Port O'Connor and Ronny Lester's fish camp. The first night was calm, and we pulled in more than eighty flounder.

About daylight a thunderstorm hit and muddied the whole bay. It stayed rough for the next two days, and the only clear water was in the new Intracoastal Waterway where we caught a few trout.

On the fourth day the sun came out, and the wind changed around noon to southeast at about five knots. We loaded the boat and hit the Middle Grounds at 3 p.m. The tide was low and running out like a millstream. Some of the area was exposed.

We beached the boat, and Wortham waded across into the surf. I stayed on the north side in calm water and saw two large redfish swimming the edge within casting distance. Both fish went for my spoon when it hit the water. The largest one got it and pulled every bit of my line to bare spool. I walked with the fish, trying to get some of my line back; but the little sport cast reel I was using couldn't stand the pressure and the spool wouldn't wind. Twenty minutes later I landed the fish hand over hand. It was well over thirty inches.

Fortunately, I had a spare reel with thirty-pound test on a Calcutta rod in the boat. I rigged a leader with a small lead sinker and tied on a black Hedden Torpedo lure. The fish turned on it like gangbusters, and we fished the rest of the afternoon standing on the exposed reef beside the boat. We caught redfish every cast and stacked them on the ground behind us. They were all over ten pounds. When we loaded the fish into the boat, it almost sank. We made it back to camp and the icehouse with eighty-two flounder and more than five hundred pounds of redfish.

Bear in mind this was the late 1940s. There were no limits and catching that many fish was standard procedure for better fishermen. Plus, we always ate everything we caught or gave to others what we couldn't eat.

We returned to the Middle Grounds during high tide at daylight the next day. The tide was just beginning to run out, and the area was covered with at least two feet of water. As low tide progressed, the currents made wading difficult. The wind was up and blowing opposite the tide, creating a rough situation.

None of this seemed to bother the fish, though. We caught thirty-seven large trout, all over four pounds, before calling it quits. It had been a very productive fishing trip. When we got back to camp, we unloaded the gear, dumped our fish into the boat, and covered them with ice and a tarp. The axle on my trailer was bending from the weight of the fish, but we made it back to Houston. That's why I remember the trip.

By the late 1950s and early 1960s, it began to get crowded around Port O'Connor, so I moved on south to San Antonio Bay and set up a camp at Panther Point.

I always fished Panther Point during the World Series. The year Ken Boyer hit the grand slam that won the series, I was making about twenty-five knots down the Matagorda Island shoreline with a transistor glued to my ear. Another October morning, on the second day of the series, Johnny Downs (founder of the Hudson Engineering Company in Houston), my friend Al Vincent (ex-manager of the Baltimore Orioles), Beamond Exporter, my cousin Erwin Grigar (whom I consider the second-best artificial-lure fisherman in the world), and myself made camp at Panther Point.

The area had become one of the most productive wade fishing spots along the coast for us. We planned to fish four days. On this particular trip we camped on the bay side of Panther Point just across from Panther Reef, which is about two hundred yards off the point. Normally we camped on the inside of the point for protection from storms; but the weather reports were good, so we stayed bayside.

We got up at 2 a.m., made coffee, eased our boat across to Panther Reef, anchored, stepped out, and waded within casting distance of the reef. The fish were there in great number. We were using quarter-ounce Johnson Sprite Spoons and had a two- to four-pound trout on every cast. By daylight we had full stringers and more than a hundred trout. I suggested we had enough for the first morning, and we returned to camp and fixed breakfast.

After breakfast we moved about ten miles toward the second chain of islands near Cedar Bayou. The first three hours only produced half a dozen redfish. As we worked our way west, we found more. I waded back to the boat and brought it forward a mile or so, anchored it, and fished forward. By 3 that afternoon we had more than fifty redfish. We returned to camp to fillet our fish. It was only the first day of a four-day trip, and we'd already filleted over 150 good-sized fish. That night we cooked fish and rested.

The next morning we returned to Panther Reef. Again, we caught over fifty trout. Same lures. Then we went to the second chain for about forty more reds. Again, we spent the rest of the day filleting fish, resting, and listening to the World Series.

By now our ice chests were full. We cut our trip short and headed back to Houston.

A southeast wind is usually a good fishing wind along the Texas coast. It brings fair tide and clean water. Personally, I like fishing in a strong northeast wind. It brings high tide, yet the water stays clear in most redfish holes. I mention this because I always liked to fish Panther Point during these winds. The only problem was getting across San Antonio Bay to the reef during stormy weather. You could swamp in a moment if you were careless. Once across, I always found good fishing action.

One November I had Carl Schwartz's party and Erwin Grigar booked for a combination duck hunt and redfishing run on Panther Point. The weather turned sour with drizzle and rain. Wind was from the northeast at about twenty-five knots. Carl called me and was very upset about the weather. I assured him it was the kind of weather we wanted, perfect for ducks and redfish alike.

The trip across San Antonio Bay was rough. Carl had about decided this was a crazy venture. Once across the bay, though, we entered the protected waters behind the point and found exactly what we were looking for—a tide two feet above normal and good, clear water. Ducks were flying everywhere since the bay was so rough, and they'd come into the cove looking for a place to land.

My camp inside Panther Point was protected from all directions. I'd weathered some bad storms there—short of hurricanes—and never endangered anyone's life or lost any equipment. The only time I came close to having a problem was the night a roar like a freight train woke me up. I jumped out of my sleeping bag and put a light on my boat. It was sitting high and dry. I'd left it anchored in three feet of water when I went to bed. A waterspout had just missed us and had sucked all the water from around my camp, leaving the boat sitting on bottom. In a few minutes the water came back and everything returned to normal.

We forgot about shooting ducks the next morning and went fishing. I dropped Erwin and Schwartz in South Lake and went to the north end of Panther Lake, anchored, and started wade fishing downwind, parallel to the shoreline. Within a hundred yards I had several large reds, a couple of saddle-blanket flounder, and a number of good trout. I began to feel guilty the other two weren't with me, so I hopped in the boat and backtracked to them. When I got within shouting distance, I cut my motor and asked if they were having any luck. Erwin answered, "You have a winch? I got so many fish on my stringer I can't lift it."

We iced over three hundred pounds of redfish that afternoon and got our limit of duck. That night raccoons got into our food and cleaned us out except for leftover duck stew. They hung around camp the next day begging handouts. They even learned how to open the ice chests. Eventually I had to build a wire cage to put our food and ice chests in.

The weather was worse the next day. We heard on the radio there were gale-force winds in the Gulf. We killed another limit of duck, iced everything down, packed up, and headed for Houston.

One other November run to Panther Point stands out in my mind. I found redfish all over the flats and reefs, and pin-tail duck by the thousands. Bob Grigsby, Earl Lingo, Jack Montgomery, and I were the only duck hunters on the lake mainly because no one had to go that far to get a limit. Plus, no one wanted to have to cross San Antonio Bay if a strong norther blew in.

Earl had made three portable duck blinds out of chicken wire and cane. The finished product looked like a natural bush, weighed only about ten pounds, and rolled up like a rope ladder. We put the blinds, some pin-tail decoys, and our fishing gear in my Boston Whaler and headed across San Antonio Bay on Friday. We planned to fish three days.

The weather was perfect when we got there. The day was mild with a light southeast wind, and the water was clear. Tide was about normal, and there was a cold front moving south about two days out. We had just enough time that evening to

Wade fishing's all-time Dream Team, a first-string lineup of level-wind talent: from left, Jack Montgomery, Charlie Paradoski, Maurice Estlinbaum, and Grigar, Chandeleur Islands, November 15, 1984. There was no limit on size or numbers of redfish. Photo by Joe Doggett, courtesy of the Houston Chronicle.

set up our blinds for the next morning. Since I always camped on Panther Point, I kept three or four crab traps out around the clock, baited with redfish heads. The first thing I did when I got there was check my traps. On this particular evening I had eighty big blue crabs, most of which I cleaned and fried for dinner. The coons picked through our shells.

The next morning Lingo went duck hunting, and the rest of us went fishing. I located the redfish on the third chain of islands about ten miles south of Panther Point. The incoming tide was perfect. They were up against the long, shallow reef for a quarter mile or more, just like they'd always been for as long as I could remember. We dropped into the water quietly behind the reef. The morning tide was perfect. I had a five-pound red on my fifth cast. Montgomery was about fifty feet to my left, and Grigsby, about the same distance on my right. We didn't move over fifty yards from our spots that morning and caught big redfish on quarter-ounce copper Johnson Sprite Spoons. We had over fifty four- to five-pound redfish in no time. When we got back to camp, Lingo told us he'd had his limit of duck in just about fifteen minutes. He was marinating sliced duck for lunch, and it was about ready for the frying pan.

These trips were typical for Panther Reef during the 1940s, 1950s, and 1960s. Always, there were abundant redfish and trout. Each time we went, with very little effort, we came away with forty to a hundred good eating six- to ten-pound trout and reds, all taken on spoons and light tackle.

I continued to fish the reef and the small islands off Port O'Connor from the late 1960s until 1975 and booked well over a hundred trips to my camp during this period.

I began to notice, however, a drastic change in the redfish population during the early 1970s. Each time I went, my party caught fewer and fewer fish. I began to notice when I was there every Sunday evening around 4 p.m., after the weekend boaters had gone, commercial netters would come into the bay and set nets in Calhoun County waters, which was legal. But they didn't stop there. They would keep on setting nets in closed waters, too.

Since my party and I always stayed at Panther Point until Monday, I began to observe the netters closely. They were taking thousands of reds daily. I began to confront them. When nothing happened, I got in touch with the game warden and began pointing out where the nets were set and, if I knew, who was setting them. There were lots of gill nets, too, which caught fish indiscriminately. Those that weren't wanted were left to die or were tossed aside.

One afternoon a group started stringing nets along one of my favorite fishing flats in waters closed to netting. When I asked them what they were doing, they threatened to kill me if I interfered with their netting operation. I told them they'd better not miss if they tried, and I got in touch with the warden.

The next time I came down, I found they'd burned my camp.

Eventually these netters picked the waters around Panther Point bone-clean of redfish, and I stopped booking trips there.

Out of curiosity, Charlie Fisher and I went back to Panther Point during the late 1970s. We took my Boston Whaler to search for redfish. The surf and weather were ideal with the wind southeast at ten knots.

We anchored in the middle of one of the best redfish flats along the Texas coast where I'd caught thousands of reds over the years. Nothing. We beat the flats, holes, and guts to a pulp with our favorite lure—the quarter-ounce, copper Johnson Sprite Spoon—and managed only seven small trout and two keeper reds. Just about enough for a good evening meal. I couldn't believe it.

The next day we moved to another spot inside Light House Cove. Again, our efforts produced only a couple of small trout. There just weren't any fish.

I'd brought along a small inflatable boat with a five-horsepower motor that could run a couple of hours on a quart of fuel. It was ideal for getting to the "Fish Pond." Professional fishermen around Port O'Connor are familiar with the Fish Pond, but the average fisherman isn't because it's hard to get to.

The pond was normally a prime fishing area and guaranteed fish. We loaded our tackle and ice chests in the inflatable and headed for the pond. After four hours of fishing, we only managed five small reds and a couple of trout and flounder. Normally I would have left the pond with the inflatable loaded with so many fish I'd have to get out and pull it back to deep water. This time it was easy coming out. In fact, it was the first time in my life I ever rode the inflatable out of the Fish Pond.

The weather turned bad that afternoon, and the rain set in—over eight inches before it was over—but the Whaler was self-bailing, and I had a good top. We cooked what few fish we had and slept dry. The weather turned clear about noon the next day. Since we had a couple days left on our trip, we began wade fishing every area I knew around Port O'Connor, including inside Pringle Lake and Cedar Lake where I've caught two and three hundred pounds of fish a night. What we caught were about four keeper reds and a couple of flounder, in all, about sixty pounds of fish for four days—and the entire area had already been closed to netting.

In truth, I'd seen the changes coming during the 1960s—more people, fewer schools of fish, smaller schools, smaller fish. I noticed the land cut and the Laguna Madre—in the past a wade fisherman's paradise—were good for a few trout and, if you were lucky, a red or two.

Anyway, I'd already found my next fishing spot in the Gulf—the Chandeleur Islands seventy miles east of New Orleans. Trout and redfish were wall to wall, and the islands were still in pristine condition.

6

The Last Great Wade Fishing Spot in the Gulf

The Chandeleur Islands are one of the last great wade fishing locations left in the Gulf. They're not overrun or overfished, and the water stays clear year round, regardless of wind direction. The fishing is always good, even when it rains. When the winds are high, the only access to the islands is by floatplane.

The islands, an unspoiled barrier chain, are located about seventy miles southeast of New Orleans and about forty miles south of Mississippi's delta. They're about four hundred yards wide and curve outward toward the Gulf like a quarter moon, thirty-five miles of intermittent sand and low mangroves about four feet above normal tide. On the Gulf side, the Chandeleurs have low, sandy beaches that stretch outward to deep water. Behind them, Chandeleur Sound, like the delta, is a maze of ponds, inlets, and saltwater marshes that hurricanes routinely flush and refill.

There's excellent redfishing in the sound and delta, too, if you know where to find them. The areas are within a federally protected wildlife refuge, made up of unstable sea-level islands formed by the Mississippi River over the years as hurricanes shifted the River's discharges into the Gulf. They're cut by deep passes and bayous full of fish, many of them saltwater fish, trapped there until another hurricane frees them. Delta fish aren't as big as Gulf fish but there are lots of them and they're scrappy.

You can find just about any southern bird somewhere in the delta, too, including the brown pelican, which is holding its own. There're also racoon and rabbit. In the winter tens of thousands of geese and duck arrive, and on cold mornings you can hear them calling for miles.

I first fished the Chandeleurs with Jack Emmott and Norman Busse one September during the late 1960s. The first ten fish I hooked were bitten off by sharks. Ten fish, ten lures, and a whole lot of line gone first rattle out of the box. I wondered about those islands.

Finally I landed five big keeper trout on the bay side that evening. That's when I discovered you could still catch and land fish from a Chandeleur beach and not have to worry about sharks. Chandeleur fish weren't spooky like those along Texas beaches. There's no traffic, skiers, or swimmers thrashing around in the surf to scare them.

A couple months after that first trip to the Chandeleurs, I asked my good friend Doctor Schumacher and floatplane pilot Steve Littleton to fly me over the islands for a look-see. A cold norther had put frost on the ground that morning. It was calm, sunny, and crystal clear—ideal flying weather with 100 percent visibility.

I saw for the first time that morning all fifty miles of the Chandeleur Islands and their surf. The water was gin clear on both the Gulf and bay sides. Steve dropped down to two hundred feet and made a pass along the shallows. I saw schools of large redfish scattered the whole length of the islands.

Because it was cold, the fish weren't moving. When we made a low pass over them, they scattered, then pulled together again by the time we pulled back. There were hundreds of channels on the bay side of the islands, all the way to the bank. Most of these channels had between five and ten schools of redfish in them.

When we flew over Curlew Island in the middle of the Chandeleur chain, I saw a tremendous school of mullet and

Plugger's original fishing shack on Curlew Island in the Chandeleurs. Hurricane Frederick would blow this shack and most of Curlew Island away during the early 1970s.

baitfish in a frenzy. There were thousands of them in very shallow water with a big school of redfish feeding on the mullet. Each time we made a pass, the redfish would scatter, then return to their feeding. I estimated around five hundred large reds in the school. I hadn't seen a strawberry patch like that in a decade.

Steve set the plane down near Curlew. We slipped on our waders, rigged with three-quarter ounce shrimp tails, and began pulling in reds with each cast. In forty-five minutes we had all the fish we could carry.

I knew, then, I was going to spend the rest of my fishing days there. I applied for, and received, a permit from Louisiana to put a camp on Curlew Island in the Chandeleurs. The island is state—not federal—property. At first, I pitched a tent. Then I began to build a good-sized shack out of mahogany driftwood I found along the beach. When I finished, I found a sign from an old shrimp boat—the *Dixie Buccaneer*—and tacked it on my shack.

The Plugger's disciples Joe Doggett and David Boyles outside the "Grigar Hilton" on Curlew Island, Chandeleur. Photo courtesy Joe Doggett and the Houston Chronicle.

Steve was flying fishermen in and out, and my guide service grew. I became friends with Louisiana's game wardens patrolling the Chandeleurs. One was Buddy Seal. He was an honest to goodness real game warden. He made sure politicians and fat cats were not given preference when he caught them game hogging. He helped keep the area around the Chandeleur Islands clean.

Wardens Seal and Gus Mauner, Littleton, and I would use a new code each week on our marine radios to communicate information on net boat locations without tipping off the netters. By doing this, the wardens were able to keep the Chandeleur Islands free of net boats for almost ten years. The wardens also used my camp to land and stay the night if needed.

This ended when Seal retired and the Wildlife boys lost part of their budget for patrolling the area.

Netters and other violators moved into the Chandeleurs each winter—December through April—and went unmolested until

"Go that way!" Grigar directs his assault team like a commando taking the Chandeleur Islands. Photo by Joe Doggett, courtesy of the Houston Chronicle.

spring when fishing season began and the sharks and trash fish moved back in.

My camp was located eight miles north of six natural gas flares. Many of my clients booked trips just to fish the flares at night.

The flares were clustered near Breton Island in sixteen feet of water. The fish would usually congregate around one or two flares during the winter, but you had to locate them. If you got there late, fishermen would be congregated over the schools.

Thousands of redfish would cluster like sardines around the flares, swimming in the light, a churning, moving strawberry patch. During summers, millions of insects were drawn to the flames. They died from the heat and dropped into the water. Bluefish, Spanish mackerel, speckled trout, and millions of baitfish would join in a feeding frenzy on the insects and each other. On top of the fish were the fishing boats and above them, sea gulls hovered eating insects and the smaller baitfish. You didn't look up.

The Last Great Wade Fishing Spot in the Gulf

Pipestems beneath the water were solid barnacles. If a fish dragged your line against one, your line, fish, and lure were gone. A good stock of lures and tackle was essential for fishing the flares.

Catching these large redfish on light tackle around the flares was a sport unto itself. We used the seven-foot casting rod and an Ambassadeur reel loaded with seventeen- or twenty-pound monofilament line. The trick was to hook the fish away from the stem of the flare, then let the fish run off about two hundred feet of line before stopping him and letting him "wallow" while we prepared the net.

I dip netted for my fisherman. When I told one to "come on," the fisherman would reel the red in fast hoping a shark didn't cut him in half on the way in. Sometimes I'd have two or three fishermen holding big reds a couple hundred feet out, waiting their turn to net. I had to net the fish first pass because if I didn't, the barnacles would cut the line like a razor; and if the barnacles didn't, a shark would have him. We caught thousands of redfish like this.

During winter months and the off-season, commercial fishermen and shrimpers with whole families on board would pull alongside the flares. Then, using slaughter poles—thick poles with strong lines and large hooks baited with small baitfish—these fishermen would catch thousands of redfish, heaving them on board just like tuna. It's difficult to estimate how many redfish were slaughtered like this around those flares. Millions would not be out of line, half of which, in my estimation, were thirty inches or longer.

The term *game hog* took on new meaning at the flares. A boat would arrive with four or five fishermen in it. A couple hours later they would have a hundred fifty or two hundred redfish piled in the boat—three feet deep.

One spring night three fishermen arrived at the flares in a twenty-five footer. They heaved so many redfish aboard that the boat sank after they left the flares. This happened just after midnight on one of those rare nights after everyone else had gone. Their radio was submerged. They tied themselves to the boat with anchor rope and clung to its side all night, drifting, praying sharks didn't get them. One man said the rosary over and over again, even though he hadn't been in church in years. They were twenty-five miles from shore, the water temperature was around fifty degrees, and their chances of survival were slipping away.

Then a miracle happened. I had to go to Houston that week, so I called a fishing buddy of mine in Houston and told him to bring some gas to my shack and stay and fish while I was gone. I hitched a ride out on a floatplane about the same time he was on the water en route to my camp, some thirty-five miles away. He set his compass on a ninety-degree heading over open water and headed for my shack.

The flare fishermen and their capsized boat drifted directly across the ninety-degree heading at the precise moment my friend crossed their path. He pulled them from the water and saved their lives. God had a hand in their rescue.

The action beneath the flares continued for some twelve years until the price of natural gas went up. The flares were shut in during the mid-1970s and the gas was piped north for profit.

I began booking trips to the Chandeleurs during the late 1960s and early 1970s, even though I still had my camp at Panther Point. The Gaidos from Galveston's restaurant family were wade fishing the shallow bar in Monkey Bay with me on November 6, 1973, when we walked into a tremendous school of trout. We caught and released more than two hundred five-pound specks on top-water lures in a little over two hours. I can't remember seeing a larger school of specks. They covered at least five acres in the shallow flats.

In 1975, the twenty-five miles of salt grass flats and surf around the main Chandeleurs were wall-to-wall fish—year round. On a cold, foggy Valentine's Day in 1976, Houstonians Earl Lingo and Bob Grigsby caught eighty-eight large speckled trout in one afternoon on gold spoons inside Hollowood Bayou. Word got around among saltwater lure purists, and I stayed

Fall was prime time to wade the green flats for redfish behind Chandeleur Island. Light-tackle strings like these were routine when the Plugger was in his element. Photo courtesy of Joe Doggett and the Houston Chronicle.

booked. One year I didn't get home to open Christmas presents until February 22. The limits then were fifty redfish and fifty speckled trout, and no one made a dent in the fish.

On Thursdays Louisiana's fish and game people—Gus Mauner, Steve Joiner, and Buddy Seal—always stopped by my camp. They patrolled the Chandeleurs by floatplanes and kept violations to a minimum.

Richard Schutte and Ron Hauser always made it to the Chandeleurs. They started fishing with me when they were in pre-med school and continued to book trips over the next thirty years after they became doctors. They never missed December 15 or the last week in February. Both of these gentlemen became top lure fishermen.

I'll never forget the year 1979 in the Chandeleurs. It started with good weather and stayed that way until June. The sound and surf were generally calm and clear. My parties caught plenty of trout and redfish. One group caught about forty real nice flounder on jig worms right in front of my shack on Curlew.

About midweek, during the first part of June, Littleton flew in a planeload of needed staples, ice, and gas for the boat. The weather was still perfect, and the sound was like a millpond.

Then, as often happens in the Chandeleurs, the weather turned bad overnight. The wind shifted out of the northeast at twenty-five knots. Waves rose, and the surf rose too high to fish. On the third day the wind calmed to around fifteen knots, and we managed the run from Curlew to the main Chandeleur Island in my Boston Whaler. We caught enough redfish and trout to salvage the trip, and my fishermen left happy.

In July, I had another group in from Amarillo and Austin. Again, the weather started good—almost too good with not quite enough wind or tide for top-notch fishing—but we worked hard and filled stringers everyday. That party left, three more fishermen flew in, and so it went. I took a break and returned to Houston July 4, then returned with my wife, Mary, on July 8.

My next party—two couples—were already there and ready to fish. The weather was perfect, and we caught several nice fish that afternoon. The next day was identical and we continued to catch fish. On the third day the weather turned bad, the tide started rising, and the wind picked up. I became uneasy.

Regardless, trout and reds were wall to wall in the Curlew surf. We were catching fish when I noticed Mary about a quarter mile down the beach waving a white towel at us. When the rain started, she'd switched on my weather radio and found a tropical storm had formed overnight in the Gulf almost on top of us.

Everyone started packing equipment. I got Littleton on the radio, and he was there within forty-five minutes. I got my couples on board, and Mary and I took the Boston Whaler across the sound to New Orleans where we spent the night.

The storm blew in at midnight with winds around fifty knots and lots of rain. I stayed in New Orleans a couple days, made a few repairs to my boat, and returned to the Chandeleurs to meet a party of five.

We caught our limits of trout and redfish along with some forty flounder. Everything was fine until their last day when Hurricane Claudette formed quickly in the Gulf. Once again we packed and boarded up. I put four fishermen on Littleton's airplane, took one with me in the Whaler, and struck out across the rough sound. Fortunately, the hurricane went in south of us.

When the Gulf calmed, I returned to find about eight hundred dollars' damage to my camp. Still, I considered myself lucky.

Fishing was bad for about ten days after the hurricane. Then, about the middle of August, the water cleared, and trout and redfish were everywhere, feeding, wall to wall.

My clients kept flying in and leaving with full ice chests. One man—an expert fly fisherman—arrived with nothing but his fly rod and tackle. I was curious to know how he would fare when he hooked a big skipjack. He did just fine.

The weather and surf were good, and trout and redfish were running a nice size. Finally I couldn't stand it. I grabbed a fly rod, and we got into a nice school of trout in the flats near Lingo Lagoon, catching them on top-water popping bugs and streamers. The fly rod felt comfortable in my hand and brought back memories of Gus Rohan and my first lessons. I enjoyed catching the specks on the streamers. The fly fishing group left with full chests and promised a return trip later in the year.

I kept hoping for a thunderstorm to refill my water containers, but they kept missing us. Often I drank rainwater when my supply was low.

Fishing was good the rest of August. Then September rolled around. I had Jerry Webb, Ken Corey, and their two sons with me. We had good fishing and caught plenty of reds and specks the first day. Then, on September 1, Hurricane Bob formed in the Gulf. I couldn't believe it. I got my clients out and closed my camp to wait it out. It wasn't a strong hurricane. The surf roared and I got some of the wind, but it passed by and went in at Port O'Connor.

When it calmed, I found damage on the east side of my shack. I lost a few things that weren't tied down. I had everything repaired in a half day. Damage came to around nine hundred dollars, but again I considered myself lucky.

In all, six hurricanes had already entered the Gulf. So, when a hurricane named Frederick formed about fourteen hundred miles to the south, I didn't pay it much attention, thinking it would be unusual if number seven made it to the Gulf. Surely the odds were against it. I called my next group and told them to come on.

We had good fishing and by Sunday morning, September 10, they had about seventy-five flounder and their limits of specks and reds all iced and ready to go. They left at noon.

I began monitoring my weather radio. The storm was on the other side of Cuba with winds around seventy miles an hour. The next morning I awoke at 3 a.m. The wind had shifted from the northeast, gusting to about twenty-five knots—a sure sign of an approaching storm. I clicked on my radio. Frederick was headed for the Gulf and gaining strength with winds to 130 miles an hour.

On Tuesday the hurricane entered the Gulf. Winds at my shack were already at thirty-five knots and expected to gust to fifty knots by Wednesday morning. Everyone in the Gulf had already left, and anyone near the Gulf was leaving. I was probably the only person left on an island in the Gulf, forty miles out and in the path of a killer storm.

I had just enough time to gather up a few things, board the shack up real tight, and get the hell out. Seas were already eight to ten feet, but my Whaler came through the sound like a champ. I made it to New Orleans in a couple hours, pulled my boat out, and headed for Houston.

Frederick crossed Curlew Island and made landfall around Pascagola, Mississippi.

I hoped, by some miracle, I would have something left. Most of the phone lines were down, but I finally got through to Dave Lambert, my good friend and pilot in New Orleans.

He flew over Curlew and could hardly believe what he saw. The island where my camp sat was gone. It was under eighteen feet of water. The nearest piece of Curlew was about a mile and a half away from the spot my camp had been. I'd lost everything.

I called Lambert back a day later and asked him if he knew of anyone with a good houseboat for sale. Once again I was lucky. Lambert had one in the water at Slidell, Louisiana, and offered it to me at a reasonable price. It was outfitted and ready to go. Mary and I got in the car, drove to Slidell, and bought it.

I knew the waterway to the Chandeleurs was navigable, but the islands were 125 miles away. Nonetheless, I needed to get there and get back in business. I'm not a wealthy man.

To get there I had to cross twenty-five miles of open water across Lake Ponchartrain, then go thirty miles up the ship channel, dodging seagoing vessels. From there I had to zigzag twenty-five miles through delta marshes and wetlands before traveling thirty-five miles across Chandeleur Sound to North Island, where I'd decided to make my new camp. The houseboat had a twenty-horsepower Evinrude. Ken Hagen made the first leg of the journey with me to Shell Beach, Louisiana. We left at sundown and traveled all night. They raised the railroad trestle for us, then we crossed under Interstate 10, pulled into a well-lit

Plugger with full stringers returning to his houseboat in the Chandeleur Islands with his longtime island companion Yakapoo. A winter storm would sink this houseboat a year later and Plugger would purchase the 56-foot steel-hulled boat Plugger *to house the fishermen he guided in the Chandeleurs. Circa 1970s. Photo by Joe Doggett, courtesy of the* Houston Chronicle.

fishing marina at 3 a.m., and went to bed before tackling the ship channel.

The next morning a man at the marina gave us good directions to Shell Beach where my son Rudy and my friend, Al Vincent, met me with my Whaler. Ken left for Austin, Al came aboard, and we got underway through the marsh.

We made it into Morgan's Harbor at the end of the next day, September 25. Beyond lay the sound and the Chandeleurs—thirty-five miles away—but the wind was blowing at twenty-five knots, and the seas were rough. We made camp inside the wetlands and started exploring the inland lakes and bayous.

We found the marshes full of lakes and oiler slips. Fish were everywhere. At night the mosquitoes and gnats were so bad it was impossible to move after sundown.

The good ship Plugger *was a comfortable base of operations during Grigar's later years at Chandeleur. Note the strings of beer cans, all of which Plugger saved to plant in the saltgrass to start oyster reefs. According to the Plugger, the Chandeleur Islands yield some of the largest oysters in the world, up to nine inches, unpolluted, and edible the year around. Note Yakapoo on watch. Photo by Joe Doggett, courtesy of the* Houston Chronicle.

The marsh lakes were primitive. We found one that looked good. The water was clear—not too deep—and alive with oysters. We slipped on our waders, fished it a couple of hours with Johnson Sprite Spoons and managed ten nice reds, all around five pounds.

That night the wind died, and we found the sound slick as butter the next morning. We set out for the Chandeleurs in the houseboat, towing the Whaler.

Not knowing the lay of the islands since the storm, we anchored behind North Island for the night. The next morning we found Frederick's waterspouts had cut several deep fifteen- to twenty-foot inlets past and through the islands. These inlets stayed loaded with trout and redfish all winter and became ideal cold-weather fishing spots. The pipeline cut was all the way through, too. We found a good cove to beach the boat where it could be faced into the wind, ideal for winter northers,

Here's Grigar in 1985 at Chandeleur, slowing down a bit but still able to wade most young bucks into the mud. Photo by Joe Doggett, courtesy of the Houston Chronicle.

which would be blowing through the Chandeleurs in a couple of months.

During this same time period my daughter, Dene (Rudyne), and son Rudy were attending college at Stephen F. Austin and sharing a mobile home in Nacogdoches, Texas. Rudyne's boyfriend gave them a small, snow-white rat terrier puppy as a watchdog.

The dog never got very big, but he was extremely acrobatic. He could jump as high as your shoulder. They named him after then-famous Hollywood stunt man Yakima Kinet, whose nickname was Yak.

When they graduated college, Rudyne presented me with Yak. We hit it off immediately. Best of all, he was house broken and had above-average intelligence.

Yak and I set out from Hopedale, Louisiana, to the Chandeleurs. We had about seventy-five miles of rough seas that day, and Yak became seasick. I didn't want him washed overboard, so I held him in my lap all the way. When we hit shoreline near my shack, he jumped out and started bouncing up and down like he was on a trampoline. He was glad to be back on land.

For the first time in his life Yak had several miles of island to roam. And, for the first time in his life, he ran across animals and birds he hadn't seen before, which also brought out his hunting instincts.

I had a pet rabbit close to my camp which I fed and had made a nest for in an old five-gallon bucket. Yak found it, killed it, and drug it back to camp to show me.

I scolded him and made him understand not to chase rabbits. He later learned to live with all the animals except one—the nutria.

Nutria became Yak's sworn enemy. He hated and fought them like a tiger at every opportunity, even though they were much bigger than he. I found him cut up real bad one day after a nutria fight. He became infected and I had to fly him out to a vet where he remained in intensive care for ten days.

Yak recovered and came back.

Another time a nutria cut Yak's throat in two places. He came dragging in and I could see his windpipe. A severe storm was blowing across the islands and all radio communications were out. I knew I had to close the wounds, so I found a needle and spool of black thread and put three stitches in each wound.

I cut the tops off two socks and made a bandage around his neck after treating his wounds with Preparation H, which I keep in my camp at all times to doctor open cuts or wounds. It's the best thing I've found. Yak healed within a week.

Plugger

Soon afterward I started calling him Yakapoo for some reason. I guess because he was so little. He and I became fast friends and he became my eyes and ears on the island. When we were on the water at night fishing or in a dense fog, he always let me know if anyone approached or we were near another boat.

My clients loved Yakapoo, and he and I starred in an episode of "Fishing the West," a national cable TV program. Yak also had over a hundred hours of flying time in floatplanes and on airlines.

Twice during his life with me in the Chandeleurs he became bored with having to stay in my outboard while my clients and I wade fished. So, he jumped overboard and swam some five miles back to my houseboat. Once there he would curl up inside one of the bumper tires and wait for me to come in. He would always be wet and hungry when we got there. Once, a passing boat saw him swimming in open water and took him aboard. Everyone knew him, and they dropped him off at my houseboat. I'm surprised a shark didn't eat him.

Yakapoo died of old age in 1987. I put up a small stone with his picture and dates on it in the islands. I imagine a hurricane has blown it away by now.

7

Oysters Teach Me a Lesson in Conservation

While the decline of the game fish population along the Texas coast got me thinking about conservation, it was the Chandeleur oysters that focused the picture for me.

I eat and feed oysters—fried and raw—to my fishermen daily. In fact, I've cultivated my own beds in the Chandeleurs for two decades and have hundreds more oysters today than when I started. What's more, I'll leave at least a ten-year supply behind for someone to enjoy long after I'm gone. And, if he isn't stupid or greedy, he can leave a ten-year supply for whoever follows him. The question is: Will he?

The amazing thing is I can leave these oysters even though *more than half of my beds are robbed regularly.* It wouldn't be so bad if the thieves would put back shells from the oysters they steal so the little oysters attached to the big oyster's shell could grow. But they don't. They open the oysters on the spot and discard the shells—little oysters along with them—onto stacks to rot in the sun. They destroy at least a times-ten factor beyond what they steal. In short, the thieves are either too lazy or too stupid—or both—to put the smaller oysters and shells back into the water so the beds can continue to grow.

Now, transfer this concept to dredging companies and commercial oyster fisheries. You'll find what's left of the Gulf's once

Afternoon's catch in the Chandeleur Islands, September 11, 1983. Bucket of oysters, lower left, were harvested from Plugger's natural oyster beds cultivated in the Chandeleurs.

large, natural, live oyster beds piled behind every commercial fish house and restaurant along the Gulf Coast, or layered beneath blacktop, or packed into shell roads throughout the coastal states. We've taken—and eaten—Gulf oysters for over a century without putting anything back. The fact we still have any oysters at all surprises me. When you're dealing with nature, if you'll leave as much as you take, there'll always be some for others. There is no better example of this than the natural cultivation of oysters.

Oysters have to be cultivated like orchids. Year in, year out. And no one—*no one*—should ever destroy an entire reef of oysters. Take some and leave some. Its like hunting quail. You always leave at least half the covey for next year's crop.

I've yet to open an oyster in the Chandeleurs and not put the empty shells back into the water with the live ones. The larger shells always have several tiny oysters attached. If put back into the water, they will continue to grow to normal size in about four years. Throw the shell on a pile rotting in the sun, and the little ones die. Even bottles and beer cans give little oysters something to attach to. I've found as many as eight large, live oysters attached to a beer can. I saved every beer can to build oyster reefs on the Chandeleurs. When I retired in 1989, I left behind at least fifteen private oyster reefs in deep water. I hope to come back one day and enjoy another super oyster meal.

Although oceanographers and marine biologists are concerned about our Gulf's resources, many tend to have built-in biases in that they often disregard opinions like mine as "nonacademic." What they fail to realize is I've been there. I've been in the water looking, watching, thinking. I'll match my conclusions with theirs any day. In truth, it's going to take a concerted effort to conserve if we're going to have anything left to fish for, eat, or write about in the Gulf.

I've noticed that oysters do not need deep water to grow. In fact, the best, fattest, and largest oysters come from soft, shallow, muddy potholes without tide circulation. Period. They grow even when the water is brackish from rainwater and runoff. They grow even when they're exposed—high and dry— for periods of time. And they will remain fat and continue to grow even if they're exposed during the hottest months—June and July. Once covered again with water, they rejuvenate and reach immense size.

During idle winter months when the tides are very low in the Chandeleurs, I collect hundreds of "runty" small oysters and replant them in shallow, proven oyster-bearing potholes in the flats. These oysters perk up immediately and in four years grow into huge, healthy oysters. I've been cultivating oysters like this for decades. We can manage our oyster resources and reap the rewards of our efforts. There's nothing complicated or academic about that. The only question is: Will we?

Plugger

8

How Greed Almost Decimated the Gulf's Redfish

Greed for the redfish focused my attention on the urgent need for game fish conservation. In fact, greed almost drove the redfish toward extinction while I was in the Chandeleurs. The catalyst was a market that went from nonexistent to more than two dollars a pound. And it happened so fast it caught everyone by surprise.

From the water, wade fishing, I watched the slaughter of redfish unfold and tried as best I could to help stop it. I reported spotter planes looking for schools of bull reds in deep water for commercial netters. I ripped out gill nets wherever I found them. I reported net boat locations. My life was threatened. But I knew if something wasn't done, the redfish would go the way of the buffalo and carrier pigeon. So did other sport fishermen. What the politicians didn't know was the economic benefits of sport fishing already outweighed those of the commercial fishing interests along the Gulf Coast. Eventually they would find this out.

I always had a special respect for fishermen that did right and acted right. But in every walk of life, there are bad apples. The same is true of fishermen—commercial as well as sport. And while commercial boats did the greatest damage to the redfish, a few sportsmen contributed, as well. The flares were a prime example.

Shallow bays at high tide always produce keeper specks and reds along the Gulf Coast if you know how to find the fish. Photo by Joe Doggett, courtesy of the Houston Chronicle.

Paul Prudhomme, a New Orleans chef, inadvertently started the gold rush for redfish in the late 1970s when he introduced a new blackened redfish recipe at his restaurant, K-Paul's Louisiana Kitchen. After experimenting with different ways of cooking the fish, he found the oils in the small (around four pounds) redfish—"rat reds" we call them—were ideal to cook using his blackened redfish method. Ironically, he found you could do the same thing with tuna, but it was the redfish that took off.

Up to this point, smaller commercial boats working the bays provided the rat reds for restaurants like Prudhomme's. The boats were designed for shallow water and seldom ventured offshore into deep water where states had no jurisdiction.

Consequently, the catch between commercial and sport fishermen—where reds were concerned—remained roughly balanced. The larger bull red breeders—thirty inches and over—were safe from overfishing. Even with heavy commercial pressure from gill nets, trout lines, and major freezes, there were always redfish to be caught. I think the population would have been okay with limits adjusted according to Parks and Wildlife surveys if the blackened redfish craze hadn't swept the United States.

But the media for some reason picked up on Prudhomme's redfish recipe, and Louisiana's cuisine, in general. Patrons started asking for blackened redfish in restaurants, and suddenly there weren't enough reds to fill the market. Per pound price for red fish at the dock shot up, the demand increased, and another American eating fad got underway. Restaurants started clamoring for redfish. Commercial fishing boats and big "netters," smelling profits, geared up to start seining the schools of big breeder (mama or "bull") reds in the unregulated deep waters offshore, leaving no way for the fish to reproduce.

In truth, bull red meat is coarse, bloody, and not as good to eat blackened as the smaller rat red meat. But they were redfish, and the average consumer would never know the difference.

Every little restaurant and country club wanted to feature blackened redfish on the menu. The demand was so great that fish houses converted large crew boats into commercial seagoing fishing vessels to net or seine the fish. They would hire spotter planes to locate the schools. The plane would radio the ship, and the ship would navigate to the spot and purse seine the entire school. These large vessels almost exterminated the entire redfish breeder stock. They caught so many and became so greedy they not only hurt themselves but put many of the small bay boats out of business as well. Rat reds almost ceased to exist.

Beyond a certain distance in the Gulf, commercial fishing vessels could do almost anything they wanted. There were no restrictions, no seasons, no size limitations. Nothing.

Some of these boats could easily handle a hundred thirty-five thousand pounds of redfish a day. When you consider the entire Gulf Coast sport fisherman's catch only averaged about a hundred thousand pounds a *year* during the 1970s, it's easy to see the impact these boats made on the population.

How Greed Almost Decimated the Gulf's Redfish

Loading the Whaler at the end of a day. Fall is the ideal season to fill stringers with specks and reds in Gulf Coast Bays. Photo courtesy of Joe Doggett and the Houston Chronicle.

I think the total redfish catch in 1980 was under a half million pounds. By 1985, the figure was between four and five million pounds—and climbing—and the redfish, like Florida's kingfish, the Atlantic's billfish, and other good-eating game fish, were in trouble. The redfish continued to decline at an alarming rate, even in the Chandeleurs.

Commercial fishing boats regulated their catch only according to what they could sell. If they could sell a half million pounds of redfish, that's what they took. Two large boats were capable of hauling in at least three million redfish a year; fleets, more than twenty million. Because the redfish is primarily a territorial Gulf-water fish, the impact of commercial netting boats was enormous; and until legislation passed, generally unchecked.

Out of this slaughter the Gulf Coast Conservation Association (GCCA) was formed.

In February 1977, a group of saltwater fishermen met at my tackle shop in Houston to discuss the decline of the redfish and the problems facing saltwater sport fishermen in Texas. We were genuinely concerned. We'd heard and read what had happened to Florida's kingfish and the Atlantic's billfish and mackerel. We wanted to get measures initiated to protect the reds and other game fish here.

This, in effect, was the first meeting of the GCCA. The group attracted influential fishermen with the financial and organizational muscle it was going to take to get laws on the books in Austin before it was too late. But the organization would draw its strength from the grass roots saltwater anglers. To this day, it still does.

When we started GCCA, everyone told us we couldn't fight City Hall or, in our case, the commercial fishing interests in Texas. Even if we got organized, they said, we would never get anyone in Austin to listen and that it would be impossible to restock saltwater gamefish—another of GCCA's goals.

They were wrong on all counts. The GCCA got organized, and after ten years of trying, they finally got the Texas legislature to declare the redfish and speckled trout were game fish in Texas waters, and made it unlawful for Texas boats to net them. The GCCA also got catch restrictions on tarpon, kingfish, ling, white marlin, blue marlin, and wahoo. And the GCCA set up the state's saltwater hatcheries for redfish and speckled trout. These activities soon spread to other Gulf states.

It is unlikely that sport fishermen observing legal catch limits could ever decimate a game fish population. A few commercial netters and vessels, on the other hand, have the capability of dragging in whole populations of fish in a very short period of time if the price is right. What saved the reds and other game fish along the Gulf Coast was the realization by politicians that sport fishing, and in particular saltwater sport fishing, had become a billion-dollar-a-year industry in Texas alone. The economical spin-offs for businesses like boat dealers, marina operators, motels, cafes, bait and tackle stores, and just coastal

The Plugger was one of the first during the early 1970s to nose-rig the 52M series Mirr-O-Lure for shallow fishing. Several years later, L&S Lure Company introduced the 51M nose-rigged series. Photo by Joe Doggett, courtesy of the Houston Chronicle.

The Plugger built his reputation on wading and casting lures for solid strings of speckled trout. Live bait was never an option. Photo by Joe Doggett, courtesy of the Houston Chronicle.

A classic shot of the Plugger, Lower West Galveston Bay, 1973. The trout struck nose-rigged Mirr-O-Lures in knee-deep water. Photo by Joe Doggett, courtesy of the Houston Chronicle.

businesses, in general, not to mention the numbers of people it affected, got their attention.

When politicians were shown these figures—the reaction often ran as high as 40 to 1 in favor of sport fishing. They saw the light.

And while it gave our trout, redfish, and a few other game fish a new lease on life, it's still just a drop of water on a hot stove where Texas is concerned.

There is another way to protect the Gulf Coast's fish. I would like to see a same limit/same law for all. Under this plan there would be no commercial license.

9

Why Texas Must Open the Laguna Madre

Many years have elapsed since the GCCA was formed and got legislation passed protecting our saltwater game fish. Yet, *compared to what they could and should be,* saltwater game fish along the Texas coast are scarce as hen's teeth, virtually nonexistent from Galveston to Brownsville.

A lot of the blame is laid at the feet of fish freezes, but that theory doesn't hold water. We've had hard freezes in the Laguna Madre before, like the one in 1951 when virtually every saltwater game fish caught in shallow water died. I was there the day of the freeze and fished at least four times a week in the Laguna and its bays for years afterward. And, yes, that freeze did hurt our game fish population. But you know what? In four years the game fish population restored itself and was completely back to normal—*even with* the commercial netting and sport pressure put on them then. In fact, we had *plenty* of fish from 1955 into the early 1970s up and down the Texas coast and the Laguna Madre.

Know why?

Because we had *at least* one—and sometimes more than one—fish pass open from the Gulf into the Laguna Madre. These passes let the tides circulate new water into the Laguna. Then the passes closed. And what we have now is a stagnant bathtub called the Laguna Madre.

Keep your rod high, work your fish in close, pick him up, tuck your rod, and either string or release. Photo by Joe Doggett, courtesy of the Houston Chronicle.

What few game fish there are that try to migrate up from the south into the Laguna are seined and slaughtered at the jetties in Mexico.

Open passes are the only solution for sport fish in Laguna waters. Then, and *only* then, will game fish return in numbers to the Laguna Madre—Texas's *only* natural fish factory. The revenues for the cuts could—and should—be derived from a tax on Texas saltwater stamps. *All* fishermen, young and old alike, should contribute to the project, because it is they and the generations to follow who will benefit.

The Gulf houses all of our saltwater game fish. Many people don't realize that game fish we catch inside the Laguna Madre's bays, bayous, and estuaries up and down the coast are only "spawners"—fish hatched recently inside the Laguna Madre, waiting to reach a sufficient size and maturity before trying to return to the Gulf.

Millions of these spawners never make it out of the Laguna Madre—and, thus, cannot function normally because there's no way for them to get out. With no outlets to the Gulf, they become trapped, adapt, and live out their natural lives as easy pickings for fishermen and inevitable victims of hard freeze, salinity, intolerable heat, and pollution in bay waters that average from only a few inches to a few feet deep.

The Laguna's barrier island—Padre Island—extends the full length of the Laguna. The island varies in width from a quarter mile up to two miles. It's composed mostly of sand dunes with a little vegetation. Most of the mainland side is made up of sparse South Texas ranches.

The Laguna itself runs 115 miles down the Texas coast from Baffin Bay to the Rio Grande at Brownsville. It averages two to three feet in depth. Parts of Baffin Bay on the upper Laguna are seven to eight feet deep. The Intracoastal Waterway, which runs the whole length of the Laguna, is the water's only deep channel. It's around a hundred feet wide and ten to twelve feet deep. But it doesn't help the Laguna's salinity or its fish unless there's a freeze, and then only if barge traffic is curtailed.

The only openings to the Gulf are the Brazos Santiago Pass, a natural pass that's jettied and deepened for navigation to Brownsville's port, and the Port Mansfield Channel, thirty-five miles north of Brazos Santiago. This channel was completed in 1957 so Port Mansfield could have access to the Gulf. Yarborough Pass, located about fifty miles north of Port Mansfield, sanded in years ago.

For starters, we must have *at least* one permanent pass open in the Laguna. The most crucial area is close to Baffin Bay—either one mile north or south of the bay. To avoid the effects of hurricanes, a pass should not be directly in the mouth. Passes should be made at the deepest part of the Laguna to ensure good circulation. Another pass should be made north of the land cut. In addition, we *must* keep Brown Cedar Cut and Cedar Bayou open.

These fish passes, or land cuts, must be dug right and jettied and kept open year round with dredging. Automobile bodies and used tires could be used for barricades. Part of the Laguna (from the land cut to ten miles north of Port Mansfield) has been dormant for years. These twenty-five miles should be allocated as a fish and wildlife sanctuary. This area—including the land cut— should be off limits to all activities: no fishing, no boats plowing the shorelines. All traffic should be confined to the canal—no exceptions.

When I first fished the Laguna Madre during the early 1930s, it was isolated. The only people along the lower Laguna then lived in small fishing villages. Port Isabel Bay was the only commercial fishing area. Pressure on the fish was minimal. Hurricanes kept the main passes along the Laguna open, and trout and redfish inside the passes were wall to wall. Swordfish, snook, marlin, tuna, sailfish, were in close to shore, or in nearby blue Gulf water, along the lower part of the coast. The average fishermen then mostly used nets, bait, and trotlines. In fact, you had to navigate the Laguna Madre during the day to avoid the thousands of trotlines—usually marked with white rags on each end—or else you ripped them out or cut them with your boat. After the Intracoastal Waterway was dredged during the late 1940s, we used it if we had some traveling to do to get to a wade fishing bay.

Zollie Taliaferro, June Beckley, and I began wade fishing the Laguna regularly during the late 1930s and were probably the first lure fishermen to fish the land cut after it was dredged. It was located about forty miles due south of Corpus Christi along the Intracoastal Waterway. Before World War II, we caught snook, now nonexistent in those waters.

Our game plan was always the same. When we fished the cut, we'd spend the first night at its mouth, then wade fish our way south towards Baffin Bay. We would drop two men while one man jumped the boat about a mile ahead, anchored it, got out, and wade fished. The other two would fish to the boat then jump it ahead another mile, and so on. It took us two to three days to reach Baffin Bay like this. We released everything under three pounds and never failed to fill our three-hundred pound Monel ice chests.

The fishing action always was good. On every trip to the land cut during the 1940s and 1950s we came away with hundreds of pounds of trout and redfish, all caught on artificial lures. We always had to cut our planned stay short because our ice chests were full by the end of the second day.

There were no houses then along the forty miles from Corpus Christi to the cut, even after World War II ended. It was during the 1960s and 1970s that people started building on the available land along the Laguna's beaches and waterways. The occupants brought with them their boomer outboards and seemed to delight in racing up and down the coast.

I saw what was happening and moved on to quieter, more isolated fishing spots. I stopped going to the land cut altogether until a couple of good lure fishermen talked me into going back with them one November during the 1980s. That time we got to Baffin Bay and bunked in a houseboat near Point of Rocks. The next morning I saw houses on every available canal dump, complete with private piers. I counted over a hundred on the way to cut. And the boat traffic reminded me of IH-10—hundreds of them coming and going somewhere. Baffin Bay had become a traffic jam.

The cut, I found, was closed—and had been for some time. We fished hard for the three days and managed three small trout and one redfish. We found the bay virtually dead. Truth is, it will remain dead unless the major passes are opened—and kept open with jetties—to the Gulf to restore tide circulation. I don't care how many fingerlings are produced for release. Unless hurricanes open inlets or flush pollution from the Laguna Madre, we're just dumping these fish into a cesspool.

I judged productivity around the cut at less than 20 percent. Plus, I was told the water temperature was hitting ninety degrees during the summers. This drives fish to deep water to keep cool and survive. If they can't reach deep water, they die. Algae, floating grass, and pollution inside the Laguna today also contribute to the decline of the fish population, and hinder fishermen. None of these things will change unless tide circulation is restored to the Laguna through fish passes.

South Padre Island's condo development is another nail in the Laguna's coffin. Truth is, South Padre Island is no longer an island. It is high-rise condominiums, hotels, and apartments along the bay and Gulf. It's elbow-to-elbow residential developments with canals for pleasure craft and commercial establishments for tourists and residents. It is people and structures where they don't belong, people and structures that could well be swept away by the surge of the next hurricane.

This development helped destroy the isolation of the Laguna and the fish in it. If people need this, they should purchase some silk pajamas, blow up a picture of the beach on their walls, and stay home. We don't have to ruin our natural resources for someone willing to fork over a couple hundred dollars a day just so they can get up in the morning, have coffee, and look out over the Gulf or Laguna. Couldn't West Galveston Island have been all the lesson we needed in over development? Gulf mornings are much finer from your tent or boat anyway.

Port O'Connor still has time to limit development plans before Matagorda Island becomes another West Galveston Beach or South Padre Island, but my guess is it won't. It will be developed for profit and sold to people who either don't understand or just don't care what they are spoiling for the rest of us.

Let me say again: The Laguna Madre, and places like it throughout the world are natural fish hatcheries for our oceans. Fish come into these places to spawn, then return to the Gulf. Efforts should be made to open the Laguna Madre with cuts and long, permanent jetties so fish can go back and forth between the Gulf and the bays. The jetties have to be there and put in right, or else they will sand in.

Then, and *only* then, will Texas's restocking efforts *really* kick in and take hold.

Such a project would not only prevent large fish kills in cold weather, but would give maturing reds and other game fish easy access to the Gulf during intolerable heat waves, periods of high salinity, or sudden freezes. It also would give the state back a tremendous natural fish factory and revenues from sport fishermen. And, pollution would at least be swept out with tides and decreased.

Today, Laguna fish cannot escape to deep water during a hard freeze, heat wave, or high salinity. As mentioned earlier, they take shelter in the Intracoastal Waterway and lay dormant during a freeze. During low tides (always two-and-a-half to three feet below normal during a hard freeze), heavy barge traffic acts like a concrete mixer on the bottom of the canal. Fish are churned to the surface, freeze, and are washed ashore.

The reason Louisiana doesn't have the same problem as Texas is because they have hundreds of thousands of acres of wetlands and inland lakes—natural fish hatcheries—with natural outlets into the Gulf and deep water. Plus, much of Louisiana's shoreline is inaccessible or hard to get to, thus eliminating weekend fishermen and development. Barring any unforeseen acts of man, these Louisiana marshes and outlets will be there forever and will continue to produce tons of fish for the state.

Plugger

Rudy with a nice red taken on a gold Johnson Sprite Spoon, an excellent shallow-water lure. Photo by Joe Doggett, courtesy of the Houston Chronicle.

Texas's Laguna Madre could do the same if it had the cuts to give its fish access to the Gulf. The Laguna, with its hundreds of square miles of marshes, could also be transformed into a big fish factory filled with speckled trout, redfish, oysters, and shrimp.

The shortsightedness of my generation and the generation that followed—along with the netters and the polluters—are responsible for the decline of the Gulf's game fish population. In fact, the majority of us old-timers felt our fish well would never run dry.

But it did.

The Gulf coastline is at an all-time low in productivity. Texas must do something to revive its treasured coastal waters, and the fish populations therein. Miraculously, the solution is at its fingertips—the Laguna Madre, comprising more than a hundred miles of shallow, grass flats harboring thousands of pot holes, a deep canal running down the middle, and the same length of pristine beach front separated from the Gulf by a sand dune. I know the Laguna Madre like the palm of my hand. There is not one foot of the west shoreline that does not bear my foot print, some places many times over. The Laguna Madre is not polluted with nasty chemicals or oil spills, it is only stagnant from being isolated for nearly fifteen years now, shut off, plugged from the Gulf, allowing no natural tide circulation. The Laguna is there waiting, a sleeping treasure, and can be salvaged and brought back to life simply by opening a permanent pass—deep, wide, and jettied—to flush out the stagnant water and restore Gulf water circulation. The Laguna Madre and Baffin Bay represent one third of the entire 365-mile Gulf coastline. Together, they are capable of producing great quantities of sea life each year—game fish, crabs, shrimp bait fish, and more—for generations to come. Further, Texas can set an example for neighboring states by allocating a portion of the Lagoon—at least twenty-five miles of the lower end, starting at and including the land cut—for a Texas fish and wild life sanctuary, protected from fishing, hunting, boat traffic, and trespassers.

10

Our Coastal Wetlands Can't Take Much More Pollution

Our wetlands are also on the decline, and they need our attention. Our wetlands are linked by canals and bayous to the coastal bays. The water levels and everything in them are controlled by the tides, especially the closer they are to the Gulf.

I've fished in and around the wetlands most of my life, and most always there are overlaps where both fresh- and saltwater fish can be taken. This is because salinity fluctuates with seasons and storms. I've caught reds and specks in inland lakes and marshes several months after a storm surge overflowed an area—right alongside bass and crappie. And even though marsh bass generally are smaller than their freshwater cousins, they're five times as scrappy for some reason. And fifty from one spot in a Louisiana marsh isn't uncommon.

If left undisturbed, a bayou can produce more than a hundred pounds of fish per acre; and adjacent backwater marsh lakes, as much as four hundred pounds per acre. I know Louisiana's wetlands are the backbone—the natural fish factories—for Louisiana's fishing industry. They cover several million acres and produce thousands of tons of fish each year. I can think of no better reason to protect these wetlands. Not only are they important to fish, shrimp, and oysters, they're important to millions of ducks and geese that winter and feed there—Texas and the other Gulf states included—and to many furbearing animals, as well as plants and other aquatics.

Many of the bayous, estuaries, and bays I've fished for years have become so polluted you can't eat the shellfish taken from them, particularly along the Texas coast.

In truth, these areas were probably being polluted as I fished them back in the 1950s and 1960s. I just didn't know it. Plus, the wetlands and Gulf could probably handle the pollution better then.

Now they can't. Like fighters absorbing punishment, many of these wetlands can no longer absorb the pollution blows from either developments or industry.

Let me give you a few examples. Take a look at the areas along the upper Texas coast that, during the early 1980s, the Texas Department of Health declared too polluted for the taking of shellfish. And, remember, this is only one area.

Chocolate Bay beyond Alligator Point was declared polluted. Anderson Ways and west of South Deer Island and North Deer Island and along the Intracoastal Waterway, plus Halls Lake, Cox Lake, Lost Lake, Lake Coma, Oak Bayou, Cold Pass, Eckert Bayou, Bolivar Roads, and the Lagoon were all declared polluted.

Everything within a half mile of the residential shores, subdivisions, channels, and harbor was declared polluted.

The area east of a line between Robinson Bayou South to the Sun Oil Cut at Marsh Point in East Bay was declared polluted. All of Horseshoe Lake on Bolivar Peninsula, Bolivar Peninsula and the Intracoastal Waterway, Lake Ijams, Oyster Bayou, Robinson Bayou, Sun Oil Cut, Mud Lake, Taylor Lake, all of Lake Annahuac, and everything inland from and adjacent to the Texas City Hurricane Protection Dike was declared polluted, plus everything inland beyond a line between Robinson Bayou and Marsh Point.

The region north of the narrowest point in Carancahua Bay and the inland halves of Turtle Bayou, Palacios Bay, and everything inland from the mouth of Zipprian Bayou and the mouth of the West Fork of Culver's Cut was declared polluted.

All of the Intracoastal Waterways, Live Oak Bayou, Caney Creek, McNeal Lake, Pelican Lake, the mouth of the San Bernard and Colorado rivers, and all waters connected to the Colorado River, south of the Intracoastal Waterway for a distance of eight hundred yards from the center of the river were declared polluted.

All area west of the Colorado River to a line drawn from west of Culver's Cut to the mouth of Zipprian Bayou was declared polluted.

All of the coastal waters in the area bounded by a line drawn inland from the mouth of the San Bernard River to a line drawn inland from the intersection of Caney Creek Cut-Off and East Matagorda Bay were declared polluted. This area includes Cedar Lake, Cedar Lake Bayou, and Cow Trap.

Change these names to those of the bays and bayous around New Orleans and you have an identical situation and so on around the Gulf. Only about two hundred miles of the Texas coast remain unpolluted, but even that is rapidly disappearing—the Victoria Canal which leads into San Antonio Bay is a perfect example—it's beginning to look like the Houston ship channel.

Port cities like Houston and New Orleans have great concentrations of industry. Coolant water for power units and water transportation is cheap around these cities. And both are surrounded by large wetlands where industrial waste can be discreetly discharged.

The wetlands are under tremendous pressure from developers, as well. Coasts are the "in" place to live. People continue to purchase beach houses, waterfront lots, and vacation homes there. All their sewage and waste has to go somewhere. Usually its dumped into the adjacent wetlands or Gulf. Treated, of course.

Florida learned the hard way that there were other things in the world besides development dollars. It drained several hundred square miles of wetlands to accomodate development. Now they're reflooding many of these same wetlands trying to put things back right. They may not be able to undo the damage.

Earlier days at Port O'Connor with Joe Doggett and a couple of good stringers of reds and trout taken near Panther Point. Photo courtesy of Joe Doggett and the Houston Chronicle.

Texas, Louisiana, and other Gulf states are making the same mistakes Florida made. Just look at the high rises, the beach front, and the waterfront homes along beaches and Intracoastal Waterways. Drain a bayou for development and you'll kill it as far as commercial or sport fishing is concerned.

Discharges of residential effluent also polluted Lake Houston during the 1980s. People in quarter-million-dollar homes couldn't eat the fish caught off their piers or waterski in the lake. If responsible officials didn't prevent what happened to Lake Houston, who's going to worry about some plant's or coastal residential section's discharging into something as remote as wetlands or as big as the Gulf?

We ought to declare a moratorium on all building in and discharges into our wetlands along Gulf shores and inlands like Matagorda Bay until we find out what's happening. Otherwise, we're going to crawl out of bed one morning and find these areas in the same shape as Lake Houston. Many already are.

Drainage or pollution of our wetlands has disastrous side effects on everything that lives there, including plants and trees. Wetlands are delicate. Life in them has relatively small tolerances toward disruption or pollution. Exceed these limits and fish, shrimp, oysters, and animals simply disappear or become unfit for human consumption as many are now.

I've seen it happen time and again.

We need to stop the runaway pollution of our wetlands. We need to stop issuing permits for housing or condo developments along our shorelines.

We need to stop it now.

II
How to Wade Fish

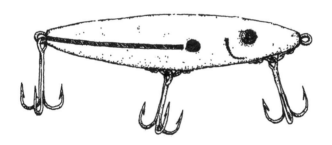

11

Support Your Game Warden

Before I get into the basics of catching redfish, I want to say a word about game wardens. In my younger days they were scarce because people believed there was no need for conservation. Game was plentiful, and ducks and geese often darkened the skies in the fall. No one thought about limits.

But even then we needed game wardens because of the game hogs. Hunters with carbide lights shot doe at night, dragged frog seines in farmers' ponds, set hoop net traps in deep river holes, "telephoned" and dynamited fish holes, shot prairie chickens out of season, and kept furbearing animals whose pelts were saleable trapped out.

This was why we needed game wardens like Bill Waddell from Austin County. He lived near Sealy, Texas, was as strict as a Texas Ranger, and kept the law tightly enforced even though he was shot at regularly by night hunters. He was fearless and always fined the violators he caught, no matter the hunter's status in life—rich or poor.

Dragnets and hoop nets were finally outlawed in the 1930s (like gill nets are today) because they were a menace to the fish. A dragnet, which was usually fifty feet long and five feet deep with two willow poles on each end, was handled by two strong men with the ability to tread water upright. A third and sometimes fourth man worked the net from behind as it filled with trapped fish. One or two passes in a private pond were sufficient to fill

These specks and reds were caught on Johnson spoons at Green's Cut near Port O'Connor in 1947.

a wagon with fish. The culprits would be gone within a couple of hours and leave behind an empty pond or lake. Pond owners countered this by planting old rolls of barbed wire in ponds.

Hoop nets were made from old buggy wheel rims with a long fifteen- to twenty-foot chicken wire pocket attached to trap the fish. The buggy wheel was the opening. Concentric circles made from the chicken wire—progressively smaller—led fish down into the trap to feed. The trap was baited with carp or other trash fish—even cornmeal—stuffed into burlap sacks. The sacks were tied down in the bottom of the trap, and the trap was lowered into deep creek holes where the current was strong. A float or cord was tied to the buggy wheel's rim to mark its spot. Large catfish would enter the trap and scavenge around the sacks.

The game hogs would ease up to the trap, quickly jerk the buggy rim up vertically, trapping the feeding catfish in the chicken-wire bottom. They dragged the trap to shore, emptied it, rebaited it, and lowered it back into the hole.

These traps produced hundreds of pounds of fish a week along a stretch of river.

"Telephoning" required an old crank type telephone. The game hogs would drop a live wire from the phone into a deep creek hole or pond and crank it to generate an electrical charge. The charge would paralyze any fish without scales. Catfish were the prime target of "telephoners." The stunned fish floated to the top of the water and were dipped up before they could regain their senses. This practice kept game wardens busy for several decades even after it was outlawed.

Dynamiting was used in honey holes along creeks and rivers. The game hogs needed an outboard motor to get away when they dropped the dynamite, though.

I witnessed one of these dynamitings in 1927 from a high bluff on the Brazos River. I was twelve years old and will never forget what I saw. Two men approached a huge hole in the bend of a river. Their fourteen-foot boat had a small outboard, the very first I'd seen. Three- to 5-horsepower motors had just come on the market. They came onto the river and stopped directly below where I was about to dive, dropped a stick of dynamite in my honey hole, motored off a short distance from the blast, doubled back, and almost sunk their boat with dead fish— catfish, buffalo, carp, gaspergous, and large alligator gars. There were hundreds of dead fish just floating away down river, wasted. (Years later I witnessed the dynamiting of fish in Mexican rivers. The fish were slaughtered by the millions.) Most were used for fertilizer.

I recognized one of the men as a constable from an adjoining county. I remember thinking he had no reason to kill so many fish—he had no children or relatives to support and lived only with his wife. He did it, I guess, for the sport, but it wasn't sport. It was slaughter. The man was later caught and prosecuted and paid a heavy fine.

Having watched game hogs like these—and later filling my own boat with reds and specks legally caught—then watching the decline of our game fish in the decades that followed, I developed an antihog attitude. I began helping game wardens pinpoint game hogs.

I helped them when I fished in the Port Lavaca and Port O'Connor areas, and every year when I fished in the Chandeleur Islands. I've run off boats purse seining reds in the Chandleurs. One large net boat tried to run me down in open water. I've also had my life threatened and my fishing camp near Port Lavaca burned to the ground because I opposed netters and game hogs (see page 56). But I believe helping game wardens is right.

One night, in 1958, my partner and I were fishing the Bolivar side of the Galveston Ship Channel. It was a dark night. Sometime around midnight, we waded into a large school of eight-pound specks and were pulling them in when a net boat pulled up within a hundred feet of us. We stood still in the chest-deep water and they didn't see us. One man drove a stake at the shoreline, then tied a gill net to the stake. The boat strung it for a thousand feet or better. We watched a few minutes, then eased over to the net and followed the boat toward deeper water, making shoestring out of the net with our pocketknives as we went. When they left, we untied both ends of the net and draped it on the highway fence—strung it the whole length of the fence—and left it there as a signal.

It gave us both a great deal of satisfaction. The netters were illegal, and we considered them the outlaws they were.

I will wage war on game hogs until I die. If you value your game fish, you should, too.

12

Shark: The Devil of the Sea

Sharks are the worst game thieves in the sea. They will take fish from your stringer quicker than the devil can take your soul. For this reason, I've always referred to sharks as devils.

In truth, these devils *are* good fishermen, but they're also gluttons and eat like there's no tomorrow. And therein lies the problem.

During the last fifty years, I believe the number of sharks in the Gulf has grown. This increase has in turn contributed to the diminishing number of game fish. Coupled with man's commercial trawlers and nets and long lines crisscrossing the world's waters today, this problem is going to get worse before it gets better.

The shark will continue to contribute directly to the problem because he has no predators. He has been virtually unmolested since the beginning and remains so today.

Adult sharks do not eat each other unless one is hurt and bleeding. Consequently, they *have* to feed on other marine life—mainly fish. A medium-sized shark will devour twenty to forty pounds of fish a day; that's about 10,000 pounds of fish a year. If this same shark lives ten to twenty years more, which he probably will, he will have consumed between 100,000 and 200,000 pounds of marine life in his lifetime. Multiply this figure by several million sharks and you get the picture.

What's left after a shark hits your fish. To prevent sharks from coming too close, keep fish on a long float stringer when you're wade fishing, especially at night. Circa 1940s.

So watch for this devil's fin in the Gulf because he loves fish he doesn't have to chase. I've lost count of the full stringers of speckled trout, redfish, and snook ripped away. On two different occasions my pants were torn away along with the stringers—by sharks smelling blood from the fish wiggling on the line behind me. Both times they bypassed me for the fish, but they scared me to death.

I've never been hit by a shark, but I've had more close encounters with them than I care to remember.

One encounter I particularly remember occurred late one evening during the 1940s. I was wade fishing San Luis Pass near Freeport, Texas, and decided to swim to a second sandbar where I noticed a flock of sea gulls working a large school of specks. I had a short stringer full of fish tied onto my pants and had started my swim. All of a sudden I noticed a large devil looking me over with two big black eyes the size of saucers—or so they seemed.

That shark was large enough to eat me and my fish. My heart nearly stopped. I untied the stringer and headed for shore. The shark grabbed the fish and seemed to enjoy the free dinner. I considered it a peace offering.

Another time I was alone snook fishing the Eighth Pass in Mexico. During low tide, sandbars would appear in the area and, from experience, I knew the fifth one up from the shore was a good place to catch fish. So, I moved out to it—about three hundred yards into the water. My stringer had about a hundred pounds of snook on it. As I reached the sandbar I saw a large shark swimming slowly in front of me. This was no harmless sand shark feeding on mullet—he was a big devil who wanted what I was lugging behind me. Very carefully I untied the stringer and literally handed it over to him.

There are ways to avoid shark attacks. My advice is to never wade fish in water waist-deep, or deeper, dressed in shorts. I recommend long-sleeved shirts and pants. A shark sometimes makes up his mind to run at something based on how it looks. Something that looks white and meaty is inviting. So, you want long-sleeved shirts and long pants to make yourself look as much unlike dinner as you can.

And if a shark gets too close and you have a full stringer of fish, simply give it to him.

On the positive side, the shark is a good fish finder. You'll find game fish where sharks congregate. So, in addition to birds, slicks, and baitfish, the shark is a fourth giveaway for game fish. When I'm fishing knee-deep flats and I find small sharks cruising the area (you can see their fins), I know I'm near game fish.

I've fished with sharks for years in the Laguna Madre—all the way to Eighth Pass—and have never had one cut at me. I've been approached by them—usually the smaller sand shark—hundreds of times while I was wade fishing. If I had just started to fish and had nothing to give him, I would make a lot of noise and stamp my feet. This seems to work. Many times sharks are just curious creatures and you can scare them off.

During the 1970s and 1980s, I flew regularly with good pontoon pilots over Gulf shallows from Port Mansfield to Mississippi. I've flown these shallows at two hundred feet when the water was gin clear and can identify any school of feeding fish clearly—trout, mackerel, mullet, redfish. In fact, you can actually see spots on redfish tails at two hundred feet.

Wherever we spotted a good concentration of feeding trout or redfish, there would always be a large, and what looked like well-organized, group of sharks outside the perimeter of the fish, looking much like sheep dogs herding a flock.

The reason they do this is the shark can't usually take a fish one-on-one. So they will go after an entire school of fish; using their speed to plow into the school, ripping into whatever fish gets in their way. They then double back, pick up the pieces, and start the process all over again. They stay with the school until they've had their fill.

I've seen this time and again during summer months with water temperatures above seventy degrees. In the fall when the water temperature drops below sixty degrees, the sharks disappear. Most Gulf sharks can't stand cold water.

Huge schools of sharks—unusual phenomena—often are sighted in the shallows off the Texas, Louisiana, and Florida coasts. Not giant sharks, but the medium-sized, two-hundred- to four-hundred-pound size. Believe me, these sharks put heavy and steady pressure on game fish. The reason for these recent sightings is they're hungry. With netters seining their schools in deep water, they come to the shallows looking for food.

From the 1930s through the 1960s, pressure on trout, reds, and other game fish was not as great as it is today; and there didn't seem to be a problem with sharks consuming fish. There was still abundance. Even the Houston Ship Channel was full of fish and there were plenty to go around for everyone, including hungry sharks.

Now there's a scarcity of saltwater game fish in many places—all trying to recover from the devastating effects of commercial netting, a growing army of sport fishermen, freezes, and now, a hungry shark population.

I declared war on sharks when I opened my tackle shop in 1975. This was before the Gulf Coast Conservation Association was founded. I had a special section in my shop for shark fishing tackle. A wholesale tackle company from New York designed and manufactured a special shark rod for me which I sold. I offered a five-dollar bounty for each shark jaw displayed, which could be applied to any shark equipment purchase in the shop. I didn't care how many jaws anyone brought in. I started the program to at least make an effort to take some pressure off the Gulf's small game fish. The program stopped when I sold my store in 1978.

Japan has a large commercial shark house specializing in shark meat which, by the way, is edible when prepared properly. Other countries are beginning to follow suit. Mankind may eventually eat everything in the oceans, including sharks. But that time isn't here . . . at least not yet.

Right now, if we're to have a well-balanced management program for our game fish, we need to deal with the shark. In fact, a shark program should be a U.S. priority—not only for its food value, but for conservation of our choice game fish as well.

Shark: The Devil of the Sea

13

Watch Your Step in the Gulf

Not only do you have to watch out for sharks when you're wade fishing, but you've got to be on your guard for stingrays. Stringrays are the rattlesnake of the sea and almost as poisonous. Fortunately, they're not aggressive and won't attack you unless you step on one. The stingray's tail is like a buggy whip—four to six feet long with a poisonous barb. He uses this barb to defend himself. Once stepped on, the stingray's reaction is lightning fast. He whips his tail around and embeds the barb in the leg or foot, usually breaking the barb off. To my knowledge, doctors still don't have an antiserum to treat stingray hits. Fortunately, they're almost never fatal.

I've been hit twice during more than a half century of wade fishing. In both instances I was careless. Both times I was walking parallel to a shoreline and not shuffling my feet. Both times the stingrays were small and their barbs penetrated my waders. Fortunately, only a small portion of the barbs penetrated my flesh. Still, the pain was like a hot iron and the swelling was terrific, lasting for nearly a week each time. Then I began to hear fishermen talk about a home remedy. Know what it was? It was everyday, off-the-shelf, grocery-store-bought Adolph's meat tenderizer.

One of my clients, a doctor from Beeville, Texas, was fishing with me in the Chandeleur Islands in 1975. A large stingray hit him just above his ankle. The barb wasn't embedded, but he was in terrific pain. I loaded him into my boat and headed for my camp. On the way I remembered I had a bottle of Adolf's meat tenderizer on board. I applied it liberally to the wound and bandaged it. Later that same day his pain was gone, the swelling was gone, and he was back fishing with the rest of the party. I've never been without a bottle since.

When a large stingray hits you direct, the barb, edged like an arrowhead, cannot be pulled out. When this happens, you have to go to a hospital to have the barb removed.

The pain is unbelievable. Usually the victim can't sleep without some type of medication. But even in these extreme cases, the meat tenderizer will work until a doctor can remove the barb.

Stingrays can be avoided by keeping your eyes open for them in clear water and always shuffling your feet. Don't high-step or run through surf. You're asking for trouble. When you see a stingray, don't disturb him. Simply walk around him and avoid any contact.

Only once did I have to get away from a ray. Early one morning in the Chandeleurs, I was pulling my boat through the shallows and noticed a wave coming towards me. It didn't look normal, so I jumped in the boat. A big ray hit the side of my boat hard. I don't know if the ray was protecting young or just didn't see me. It never happened to me again.

14

Boats for the New Breed
of Wade Fisherman

When I started fishing the Gulf during the early 1930s, racing boats were only sixteen feet long. They were mainly clinker-type boats made from planed mahogany planks with multiple oak ribs, which were heated in hot oil and shaped and bent to form a mold. The narrow boards were lapped over and bolted to the oak ribs. These boats, popular models of the day, were designed to work or "breathe" with the impact of waves in rough water. When you stored the boats for long periods of time in dry weather, they would leak like peach baskets until soaked in water, which expanded the wood and made the boat water-tight. Before a fishing trip the boats had to be water-soaked the night before and made ready. I finally wore out my first home-made skiff—a sixteen-footer. So, I plunked down my money for one of the early saltwater clinkers. But I didn't want a floor model. I needed one I could take out to bay reefs and nap in when the fish weren't feeding.

Helton Boat Works in Houston was the largest supplier of clinker boats at the time. I special-ordered a one-of-a-kind sixteen-footer. The planking was of one-half-inch instead of three-eighths-inch wood. A special tool was developed to groove a track in each board. I had them fill the groove with a flexible rubber compound that made the clinker waterproof, wet or dry. Then, I put on a 33-horsepower Evinrude engine—the first of its kind and the largest outboard then available for small boats (until then, 22 horsepower was the biggest you could buy). My clinker and I were ready.

There are several things to consider when buying a boat, including price, size, and design. The most important consideration, however, is safety. Look for a boat that will not sink under any conditions—even when swamped or capsized. Make sure it has plenty of flotation, no matter how much rain, spray, or swells get inside or wash over the boat. You want the boat to be a self-bailer with a floorboard above the waterline and automatic or natural drain features. You also want your boat's electrical equipment high enough to stay dry so you won't falter in high seas.

Serious wade or drift fishermen—because they work hundreds of miles of shallow water and grassy flats from the Laguna Madre to Aransas Pass, Rockport, Port O'Connor, Louisiana's wetlands, and Chandeleur Islands to Florida's Everglades—must have a special type of boat. Airboats, which can operate on wet grass, will get the job done. Their drawback is the noise, which scares the fish.

The early 1970s models of the Boston Whalers were ideal wade fishing machines. They were easy in and out of the waters, yet were very seaworthy in rough seas. Out of this series emerged the low profile Scooter boats with their flat, wide beams, zero freeboard, and good comfort and safety.

For the serious wade fishermen—the pure plugger—and for fishing guides that have to cover large areas to find fish, I recommend one of these or one of the new self-bailing, low-profile Scooter boats with "tunnels" that allow the engine to be set much higher than traditional hulls.

There are many models from which to choose—sixteen- up to twenty-three footers. I prefer an eighteen-footer with at least an eight-foot-wide beam and V-bow (to displace most of the spray in the heavy seas and soften the ride) and an outboard around 100 (90 is okay) horsepower to keep the weight down at the stern.

These boats can get on a plane in less than fourteen inches of water. They have a very flat stern so you can operate in extremely shallow waters, a center console mounted high, plenty of dry storage, an easy takedown convertible top, plus easy in-and-out features. A heavy-duty, twenty-four-volt trolling motor for drift fishing is also a plus. This will give you an overall safe, fast, and seaworthy boat that will allow you to cover a larger deep bay, yet still operate in very shallow waters.

15

Rules of the Road in the Gulf

Once you've purchased your boat, get licensed and take a boating safety course with the U.S. Coast Guard.

Bad judgment—sometimes caused by alcohol, bad weather, and engine failure—causes more boat disasters and deaths among boaters than anything else. This is why the "Rules of the Road"—Coast Guard-approved boating equipment and rules—are important. Keep your boat in good condition and make sure it's Coast Guard-inspected. Always have on board a good, waterproof survival kit—including flotation devices you can get at quickly—plus food, matches, water, rain gear and extra clothes, even if you're only going a short distance offshore or into a marsh.

We were experiencing a beautiful Indian summer in November 1957. The weather was in the seventies, but reports were coming in saying a cold front was due sometime during the night.

Captain June Beckley and I anchored for the night in a protected cove on the northeast shore of Chocolate Bayou. We'd never anchored there before. The winds came up, the temperature dropped rapidly, and the rain started. From our location we spotted a faint flashlight beaming an SOS from somewhere deep inside the marsh behind us. We judged it four to six miles away in the wetlands. We knew it had to be a boat because there was no way anyone could have walked there. It was about 10 p.m. There wasn't another soul within twenty miles. Beckley and I knew the area and pinpointed the signal to somewhere up Mustang Bayou, right in the middle of goose and duck country.

We dressed in warm clothing and rain gear and worked our boat five or six miles inland into Mustang Bayou. The signal had long since ceased, but we had a hunch where it had come from. When we got there, we searched for an hour or so until we found a small boat with two duck hunters lying in the floor.

They hadn't taken a survival kit with them. They had very little life left and were almost frozen to death. Their outboard had failed the day before, and they'd been without food, water, and shelter for some twenty-four hours. They'd given up any rescue hopes. We towed their boat fifteen miles back to camp and gave them hot food and blankets. Carelessness and not thinking ahead almost cost the two men their lives.

Another time two couples and a small boy came for a week-end duck hunt near my fishing camp on Panther Point. The husbands—experienced fishermen and hunters—had to be back at work on Monday. A cold front blew through Sunday afternoon with gusts to thirty-eight m.p.h. and chill factors to minus ten degrees. Against my protests, they left in three boats trying to cross the bay. After they left, the rest of us went to work on a pot of duck-gizzard stew. Later that evening, all five walked into our camp almost frozen. Their boats had capsized in the bay. They'd lost their camping gear and had no matches. Luckily for them, it was low tide and they were able to touch bottom and stay afloat until they could get back to shore and my camp.

We found them warm clothing, fed them a hot meal, and made room for them in our camp. Their boats later floated ashore with the incoming tide, and we were able to right them. A day later the wind ceased, and we towed them and their boats back to Seadrift.

Once again, poor judgment (by not waiting for the weather to calm) and poor preparation almost cost five people their lives. If the tide had been up, they would certainly have drowned. And if my camp hadn't been there, they might have lost their lives to hypothermia.

Gulf water is always dangerous, even on a beautiful day. One sunny summer day in mid-August 1976, on the Chandeleur Islands, the weather suddenly turned squally. Suddenly, a waterspout with winds of up to eighty miles per hour touched down from an ordinary dark cloud, catching many small boaters by surprise. Several drowned, including the captain of a vessel from Mississippi, who was attempting to rescue his clients. An afternoon thunderstorm in the Chandeleurs wasn't unusual, especially with temperatures in the nineties. But on this particular afternoon, a dark cloud formed and quickly covered a large area with rain, lightning, and thunder. Within minutes, wind gusts were hitting sixty m.p.h. I've seen this happen time and again without warning in the Gulf; and it almost always happens during hot, calm weather; a time when the average boater wouldn't anticipate violent weather because the day always starts out clear.

In just a few minutes the seas near my camp were ten feet. I was located on Curlew Island with my wife, Mary, and two high school kids from Houston. A boat near my camp had anchored for the weekend. The two fishermen in it—friends of mine from Mobile, Alabama—were taking a siesta in the heat of the day. They had their boat anchored at the stern. When the squall winds hit, large waves washed over the boat from the rear and sank it within minutes.

The two had life preservers on board. They slipped them on, and I could see the orange jackets rolling in the big waves as they clung to the capsized boat. As there was no way I could get to them in my skiff, I radioed the Coast Guard. My signal was faint, but they heard it and sent a scout plane over the area. They located the swamped boat and men, sent a rescue helicopter, dropped the basket, and rescued them. My wife and I got a warm thank-you message by radio. Their life preservers saved their lives because no one could swim in that kind of sea.

The Coast Guard said when they flew over our area, they saw several more swamped boats with people clinging to their sides or hanging onto driftwood. Some had life jackets, some didn't. Some drowned.

A sailboat on the Gulf side of Curlew Island washed aground, and the two people manning it were swept overboard. I'd started walking the shore with a lifeline and preserver and spotted them drifting together in their life jackets. High winds and strong currents were carrying them back toward the Gulf and deep water. My legs were in pretty good shape from wade fishing all those years, so I waded into the rolling surf trying to catch up with them. Finally I got close enough to heave the line toward them. A wave carried it within their reach. I towed them over a mile back to shore and safety. I thought I was in pretty good shape, even at sixty-five; but I was worn out fighting currents and waves and had to drop down to get my breath and let my heart quit pounding once I got on shore.

The squall continued to wreak havoc. It caught several party boats and fishermen in small skiffs—many without jackets—around Monkey Bayou. They all capsized. Many drowned, including the captain of a party boat. Understand, this was not a hurricane, but rather a routine summer squall with extraordinarily high winds.

If you're ever caught in a squall like this or see one coming, head for the nearest shore or shallow water and stay put until the seas subside. *Do not try to outrun a sudden squall.* Often they'll cover a much larger area than you can see, and you might boat yourself right into the roughest part.

Besides hurricanes or sudden squalls with gale-force winds, nothing is worse than trying to operate a small boat in a dense fog without radar. It's impossible, and you'll lose yourself quick. Sit tight if you're ever caught in it.

One day during the winter of 1978, around 5 p.m., two strangers walked into my camp at the Pipeline Cut on Chandeleur Island. They were Bob Marshall, sportswriter for the *New Orleans Times Picayune* and one of his co-workers. This was how Bob and I met and became good friends.

Plugger

They'd planned an overnight fishing trip to the Chandeleurs and were dropped off at an oil platform by the crew boat *Well Runner* out of Hopedale, Louisiana. They had camping gear, food for a day, and a small skiff with an outboard to get into Monkey Bayou.

They set up camp on the island there. Then fog rolled in so thick you couldn't see your nose. It was like this for thirty-six hours. Sometime during the night, squall winds blew their small tent away. Still, they had their skiff and were high and dry. The next day they ran out of food, but even then were not in real trouble. What they needed was shelter, something to eat, dry clothes, and a marine radio to report they were okay. They started walking along the island, and that's when they stumbled across my camp.

When the fog finally lifted, I radioed the *Well Runner* to pick them up and everything turned out fine. The point is they kept their patience. They used good judgment and didn't try to head for mainland in the fog. If they had, the winds that night would have swamped their skiff; and the story might have had another ending.

Another rule of the road in the Gulf is, "When in doubt, investigate." Never, never look the other way if you feel someone might need help. Find out. And do your best to help if they need it. And if you're not equipped to help, say someone needs a new battery for their boat, then notify someone who can tow them to shore or shallow water. A boat without a battery or good anchor may not seem like a big deal on a sunny day, but that same boat will become a deathtrap in a sudden squall or thunderstorm.

Any boat over sixteen feet should be equipped with an anchor weighing at least twelve pounds. I recommend the thirteen-pound Danforth anchor—or a close replica—which can be purchased at any marine store. I've fished through many storms in the Breton Sound flats—with winds at least fifty m.p.h.—tied to a Danforth anchor on about a hundred feet of line. Each time it held fast.

Good sportsmanship and courtesy also apply. Never run your boat close in or through another person's fishing area. Instead, slow down and circle wide and away when you come upon someone wade fishing. Keep plenty of distance between you and another fisherman. In other words, find your own fishing spot. And if you're not familiar with the area, hire yourself a good guide and let him put you on the fish.

I hold a captain's license for vessels up to one hundred tons, something not easy to obtain. I've been responsible for people on my big boat as well as the boat's safety—its safety equipment, and its operation. I have never taken my responsibilities lightly. You would do well to do the same when fishing Gulf waters, whether it's just yourself or with three or four passengers. Assume responsibility: use good judgment for yourself and them, as well. During a lifetime of fishing in Gulf waters, I've seen and known of lots of people in the Gulf who didn't. Many of them paid for their poor judgment with their lives. Some I was able to help. How many, I don't know. The Coast Guard, which rescues people everyday in Gulfport, Mississippi, thanked me officially one year. I concur with all of their rules. They have them for a reason.

16

How to Find Saltwater Game Fish

Besides sand sharks (see Chapter 15) and schools of baitfish rushing through the water, fish slicks and birds feeding are two other giveaways that you're near saltwater game fish. Plus, there are several other techniques you can use to locate fish.

Fish the "Slicks"

Saltwater fish eat each other and most anything that won't eat them first. Redfish, speckled trout, gafftops, you name them, are all gluttons and seldom quit feeding. I've caught them on lures with small fish still sticking out of their mouths. Because of this many game fish in the Gulf's bays have to clear their stomachs so they can continue feeding. When they do, they create a fish slick, and *fish slicks are a dead giveaway when you're looking for fish.*

A slick always means there are fish around. The trick is to pinpoint their location.

Here's how: When the wind is blowing from a certain direction, a large fish slick will move with the wind, *meaning fish are no longer anywhere near the slick.* The large fish slick tells you only that it originated somewhere upwind. To find the concentration of fish go upwind, make a wide circle, and look for fresh slick.

Fresh slicks will be somewhere between the size of a half dollar and a saucer. That's all. It starts small, begins to spread, and becomes larger and larger as it drifts further away. *You will find the fish under the small slicks.*

If the water is over four feet deep, circle and make a drift. Keep a buoy handy to pinpoint the slicks. Put it out when you find them and periodically check the area for other slicks. Then come back, pick up your buoy, and catch fish with your lures. Stay a couple hundred feet from the slick and fan the area with your casts. The trick is not to cast too close to your previous cast until you've located the fish. Imagine your rod as a pointer looking for fish each cast. Work it out. You'll find them. If the water is too deep to wade fish, make several drifts over the slick area.

Watch the Gulls

A concentration of gulls dive-bombing an area is a dead giveaway there are game fish working below, pushing shrimp and baitfish toward the surface.

Two or three gulls will spot a hot area like this. And within minutes twenty or thirty others will be there, all of them snapping up shrimp or pieces of baitfish at or near the surface.

When this phenomenon occurs, troll as quietly as possible within casting distance, stop all motors, and put your plug right among the gulls. Use a deep-water lure if you're in water four feet or deeper.

Jump Fishing

Here's another effective way to find fish in the shallows. Let one or two fishermen out offshore. Then swing the boat in a wide arc out away from them so as not to spook the fish, anchor it two or three miles ahead of the fishermen you let out, drop into the water, and fish ahead. (See page 90 for a more detailed discussion of jump fishing.)

The first two fishermen fish their way to your boat, load up, ice their catch, swing wide so as not to disturb your fish, and jump the boat ahead again two or three miles.

When you're fishing a shoreline or area you're unfamiliar with or you want to save time and energy during either day or night fishing, try this variation of jump fishing. Run your boat parallel to the shoreline for a quarter mile or so, then cut your motor and sit quietly. Watch or listen a while for mullet running. You may have to travel six or eight miles like this before you find them; but without the baitfish, you're wasting your time.

Once you locate a school of baitfish, start your jump. Let half of your fishing party drop into the water. Circle about a mile in front of the baitfish and leave the boat for the first group to fish to. Always leave a marker light on your boat if you use this technique at night.

Fish the Points

Saltwater fish, like freshwater fish, favor structures such as points, grassy flats, shell reefs, sunken ships, artificial reefs, or offshore platforms. These places almost always hold baitfish, shrimp, and crabs, and are natural dinner plates for feeding fish.

Consequently, a good game plan for two fisherman is to work at least nine or ten points in a bay right at daylight. Hit these places fast and spend no more than fifteen to twenty minutes at each one unless you find a good concentration of fish.

To fish a point, beach your boat about two hundred yards away so you don't disturb the fish. Each fisherman takes one side of the shoreline and works their way out to the point. Fan your side of the shore with your casts as you work toward the point. Catch what's there, get in your boat, and hit the next point. It takes less than two hours to hit several points in Galveston Bay. This routine, called bird dogging, is a sure shot for several good-sized fish as well as flounder. To catch flounder, cast your lure close to shore. Grassy points are natural flounder places.

Surf Fishing

A surf is one of the most beautiful places in the world. When the sea is calm and the water is clear, it will always produce game fish simply because fish stay in the Gulf year round. It's their home. They come into the bays to spawn, then into the surf at high tides to eat and survive.

The surf, like anywhere else, will consistently produce fish in certain areas if you know where to fish. Usually you'll find it rough with the tide's moving in or out at a fast clip. So, prepare to do some wading and work.

To wade fish a surf right, you'll need to cover at least five to ten miles a day. And, you may have to drag a heavy stringer back to your vehicle. If you do, save your catch and your back and float it behind you in the surf. Begin by working parallel to the shoreline. Look for baitfish action, sand sharks, shell banks, channels gouged out by hurricanes, or a "lagoon." A lagoon in this case will be between a deep gut (natural trench) directly along the shoreline and a second gut/bar combination farther out that breaks incoming wave action.

At high tide you'll find fish right next to the bank in the deep gut. They can be taken from shore. Many fishermen will see the second gut or bar farther out and will wade out to fish it. When they do, they wade right past fish.

The beach along Mexico's Eighth Pass and the fifty miles of Chandeleur Island shoreline are two of my favorite places. They're still pretty much in their native states—without automobiles or swimmers—and you can find deep guts running near their shorelines.

Drift Fishing Open, Grassy Flats

This style of fishing is very popular around the Chandeleur Islands. Hundreds of fishermen in small boats can be seen on weekends and holidays drift fishing the Chandeleur's grassy flats, most in comfortable swivel seats with an icebox beneath their feet.

Generally this type fisherman exhibits little knowledge of finding fish. They'll drift around until they see a boat anchored and fishing in the distance. Then, as soon as they see a bent rod, they'll bunch up around the boat, spooking away the few fish in the area. Some will even motor right through the middle of your area instead of having the courtesy to make a wide circle and come in upwind.

Wade fishermen attract these weekend drifters as well. A pair of wade fishermen working offshore in the Chandeleurs will draw every boat in the area if they see a bent rod. Again, they'll come roaring up and scare the fish away.

To counter this in a crowd, learn to land a fish without bending your rod. Once you hook your fish, keep your line tight with one hand and go through the motion of casting with your other. Play your fish down and keep it from surfacing. When the fish has played out, reel it flat in and string it underwater.

You can use a similar technique when you're drift fishing in a crowd. Stay seated when you hook a fish, keep your rod down and flat, and play the fish until you can pick it up without a landing net. Then, ease it onto your stringer without hoisting it for every boater in the area to see.

The best way, though, is to isolate yourself from other fishermen and find your own fish. Try not to barge in on someone else's fishing hole. If you need help locating fish in a place like the Chandeleurs, find yourself a good guide and learn a few tricks of the trade through trial and error.

Here's why. The main Chandeleur Island is about twenty-five miles long and has a continuous grassy flat around it. In some places the flats stretch outward a mile to deep water. At one time fish covered these flats wall to wall. Now they don't. You'll find stretches of three and four miles along the Chandeleur's shoreline with no fish. Consequently, it's easy to waste your time and energy—especially wading—looking for Chandeleur fish without knowing where to look.

How to Find Saltwater Game Fish

Again, to locate fish in a huge grassy area, watch for baitfish, slicks, gulls feeding, and sharks.

Once you locate fish when you're drifting, and if it's too deep to wade, have a small buoy ready to mark the spot. Then, make several drifts over the area. When action slows down, try another place.

Potholes in Grassy Flats

Potholes in grassy flats are sure shots, as well, even if you don't notice slicks and baitfish. The holes are very boggy and hold small shrimp and crabs that bury themselves in the mud trying to hide from predators. This is especially true in deeper water.

Learn to look for these potholes on clear, sunny days in clear water when the sun is directly overhead. In some cases, a large pothole may be ten to twelve feet deep, surrounded by grass in water four to five feet deep. Look hard for them and mark where they are. *During low tides, these potholes are usually loaded with fish.*

To fish a pothole, anchor your boat upwind, make long casts beyond the hole, and retrieve over it.

17

Good Guides Are Worth the Money

If you're going to an area you know nothing about, hire a good fishing guide the first couple of times out. A good guide is like a minister or priest. He has to have a calling or vocation for the sport—born to it, I like to believe—and a natural ability to find and catch fish.

Fancy gear and boats with bars in them don't make a fishing guide and neither does someone who decides "he'd just like to try it for awhile" after quitting his job. In situations like these, all you have is an amatuer leading a hopeful.

There's a lot more to successful guiding in the Gulf than a few years experience. You have to know the waters and the bottoms where you fish. You have to be familiar with every marker, reef, and point, and every piece of shoreline in case your party finds itself in trouble during sudden squalls, fog, or waterspouts.

A good fishing guide will have a radar picture in his mind of where he is at all times and what he's going to do if danger develops. Why? Because the people in his party are his responsibility, and their lives are in his hands. I think every fishing guide in the Gulf should be required to pass the test for licensed captain of a vessel. This certification would grind into their heads the importance of safety on the water and the fact that maritime law requires it. Many people—guides included—

become complacent or lax when fishing in the Gulf, forgetting the Gulf can kill you quickly if you're careless.

A fishing guide is responsible not only for finding fish but setting a good example, as well as enforcing the laws of the land and practicing conservation for and with his clients. Game hog days are over. Money does not buy a person the right to load a boat down with illegal fish. I don't do it, and I won't let someone fishing with me do it. It's not right, and it's the fastest way for a client to find himself on his way home.

Many guides continue to let their fishermen do things like "cull fish" as they go. The problem with culling a smaller fish off a stringer after he has been on it a few hours is that he'll die when he's released. The time to release a fish is when he's reeled in the first time, and then only gently. This is another reason I insist on single-hook lures for my fishermen. Today you don't need three hooks to catch a fish. No one does. My rule is once a fish is strung, he's yours and part of your limit.

When tides and weather are right, I find my clients their legal limits within a few hours. It's always tempting for them to want to stretch it, but I point out why it's better not to.

Still, there are those who think their money buys them the right to unlimited game fish. A party of three landed at my camp one noon. By 5 p.m. we'd caught 180 redfish. The limit at the time was fifty per day, and I told them we had enough. They became angry with me and threatened to leave. I offered to call the floatplane for them.

I took another party to a good cove and we got into a large school of reds, landing more than eight hundred pounds of eight- to ten-pound reds in a couple of hours. I began to worry about getting the five fishermen *and* the fish back to my houseboat without sinking. So, I shut it down. On the way back, one of the men kept asking me to find him another honey hole. He was still ready to fish. I couldn't believe it. He was standing knee deep in redfish and wanted more. I refused to book the man again.

Guiding wade fishermen in the Gulf has been one of the great joys in my life. I'd wager that more than 95 percent of all the people

Plugger

I ever fished with were outstanding sportsmen. They observed their limits, left the guide alone, and pitched in and lent a hand when needed. Many of my clients have been coming back for thirty years.

Newcomers, not knowing the tides and the weather like I do, often don't understand why I won't fish all day. I just tell them to wait, to be patient. Nonetheless, I keep a small skiff available at all times to accommodate these people if they insist on going out to throw blanks.

Strict, small limits of specks and reds are the rule in Texas, Alabama, and Florida. Louisiana still has a generous daily limit for sport fishermen. The state also permits one large oversized red. I oppose this and will not allow a single large "mama" red to be killed because one of these mamas will produce thousands of fingerlings, of which only about five hundred survive to maturity.

In more than half a century of daily saltwater fishing, I've yet to wade into a school of reds that numbered more than five hundred.

I saw and fished hundreds of these schools during the 1930s, 1940s, and into the early 1950s in places like West Galveston Bay and Port O'Connor.

Early one very calm September morning during the 1940s, I observed five schools of redfish within the same area near my boat. Each school had about five hundred fish in it—some in the eight- to ten-pound range, some in the four- to six-pound range, and so on. Each school stayed together. They did not mix.

After hatching, most saltwater game fish move into the Gulf and wander. When the time comes for them to spawn, they are able to find their way back to where they were born by instinct and smell. In years past, I observed that a hatch stays together throughout its lifetime. The fish stay together when they travel into deeper Gulf water. Each time the fish return from the Gulf to the bays they are a little larger.

You will never see schools like this today. And it's very rare if you see a large school at all anymore. Schools of redfish today average fewer than fifty fish, with twenty-five usually the rule. The last large school of reds I observed was in the Chandeleurs in 1986. I estimated about three hundred in the school.

A final word about guides and honey holes. Good fishing guides have their own honey holes or places where they know they can catch fish. Mine stretch from Brownsville to Alabama. When conditions are right, I'd bet anyone his month's salary I can go to any one of them and catch fish.

Time and conditions, however, change from year to year, and honey holes change with them. During the late 1940s I had a spot in the Laguna Madre near Corpus Christi. I'd pitch a tent at the edge of the King Ranch shore and run the shoreline about five miles to the Red Windmill. I'd anchor, drop into the water and wade fish back down wind, always stringing at least twenty-five to forty reds. I fished this honey hole for more than seven years until the land cut was opened. Then the land cut became one of my finest honey holes. The only thing it produces today is a long boat ride.

Generally, saltwater honey holes are usually large coves, guts, or channels that run close to shore with the tides. These channels act as funnels for baitfish, and will exhibit extraordinary tide movement. The tide will come through the channel much stronger than the shallows around it. And when it recedes, will empty strong as well. The fish, however, are in no hurry to leave and will stay in these guts as the tide recedes until instinct tells them they're about to be trapped in the shallows. These types of honey holes change with each hurricane.

Long, grassy points that extend a couple of miles into bays are also honey holes. But you have to know where the fish will be in relation to the tides.

In June 1975, I pulled alongside a party boat from Biloxi, Mississippi, anchored in the Chandeleurs. They told me the fishing had been poor and were all complaining, about "poor conditions." I told them I'd bet any one of them ten dollars I could take them to a place and catch a nice redfish in less than six casts. They almost sunk my boat jumping on. I put six fishermen in my Boston Whaler and headed for "Raborn's Point," a grassy flat I'd named after one of my fishing companions who'd passed away. It had been one of his favorite spots. When tides were right, I knew where the fish would be. And the tides were right.

We drifted in close. I dropped into the water while my six spectators sat in the boat. On my second cast I caught a red over seven pounds. They bailed out of my Boston Whaler with their rods and started casting. I pocketed sixty bucks.

Another one of my holes in the Chandeleurs is about a mile from where I anchor my houseboat, the *Plugger*. It's inside Schooner Harbor, and I can look out my window and see an area where I can catch fish anytime.

I had a fishing buddy who used to drop by the *Plugger* every once in a while and leave a bottle of dark rum, which I'd sip on in the evenings after my fishermen had gone. I finally broke down and showed this fellow my hole in Schooner Harbor. Now, hardly a day passes I don't look out my window and see someone fishing my old honey hole. I guess it's everybody's honey hole now. It was the last time I ever showed anyone one of my holes. I still have some in the Chandeleurs I take my clients to from time to time. And a few I only fish myself on days when no one's around.

18

Fish with the Tides

I've been asked a thousand times: When is the best time to fish? Dark nights? Moonlit nights? Storms? High tide? Low tide?

There is a direct relationship between tide movement and good fishing. The best wade fishing begins when the tide reaches its high, for two hours after high tide, and with the outgoing tide. Fishing during this period is especially good during stormy weather at night—the darker the better. Instinct is driving baitfish away from the predator game fish, and they head for the flats and grass during high tide.

So, don't leave the docks without knowing your tide schedules and weather conditions. Many fishermen get up early and go fishing without ever checking either. They wear themselves out. And when the tide is right to catch fish, they're usually back at camp.

With the incoming tide, it's sometimes difficult to read the water and spot baitfish. But at high tide both bait and game fish are in the flats, and that's where the action begins. Then, when the tide starts to fall, game fish increase their pressure on the baitfish. That's when you'll see and hear more and more schools of baitfish breaking the surface. They know the water is dropping, and they're forced to head back toward deeper water and leave the flats. As the tide starts out, game fish put on the pressure. Baitfish get nervous and panicky, rushing through the water, breaking the surface. Some of the best fishing action occurs during this period because baitfish are a dead giveaway for the game fish feeding on them.

Knowing where to find fish during high tide is also a key. One time a large party tried to book a fishing trip with me in the Chandeleurs, but my schedule was full. So, they scheduled a four-day trip with a fishing boat out of Biloxi. I was scheduled to rendezvous with them the afternoon of their first day. I told them when the tides were right I'd take them to a flat and guarantee them wall-to-wall reds and their limits within four hours. I picked them up around 4 p.m. that first day and headed for a small sandbar close to Curlew Island. I cut my engine about seventy-five yards out, told them to stay quiet, and drifted over the bar in about eighteen inches of water.

The tide had just started out when we got there. I eased my anchor in, and the fishermen just stood and stared at something not too many men had ever seen. Redfish were feeding, wall to wall, around the boat, their spots and tails clearly visible.

The fishermen all had their limits within four hours, meaning all the redfish they caught during their remaining three days would have to be released. They griped about it all the way back to their boat, but they didn't sound too convincing to me.

One more tide story. A party from Brenham, Texas, joined me on April 29, 1986. They landed at my camp at noon. High tide was scheduled for 2:30 p.m. At 2:15, we anchored close to one of my honey holes and waded into one of the largest schools of redfish I'd seen in awhile in the Chandeleurs. The catches were all nice keepers around nine pounds. I've done this thousands of times.

Between 1981 and 1989, the tides in the Chandeleurs have lost two to four inches of water. I've measured tides with a tide gauge consistently during my eighteen years in the Chandeleurs and noticed the low tides getting lower and lower during these eight years. Grass flats once covered with water now are high and dry during low tide.

Fish with the Tides

135

We've lost water at a fraction of an inch a year over the last eight years in the Chandeleurs. I don't know where the water has gone or why this phenomenon has occurred.

For the serious fisherman I recommend Frank Noble's "Prime Time Fishing Forecast." It includes the tides, lunar cycles, plus other information geared for fish. Noble puts this information into a computer and produces what he calls his "Prime Time Forecast." I've found it to be accurate.

For Noble's information, write to "Prime Time Forecast," 4722 Co. Road 459D, Freeport, TX 77541; or call, (409) 233-7539. Well's "Fishing Time Tables" also are accurate.

19

How to Wade Fish a Shell Reef

The best time to wade fish a shell reef is with the tide moving, preferably at night. As the tide moves in and out, fish follow it. When they hit the reef, they have to go around it. This makes the ends of the reef your best fishing area with the tides. I've found that one end of a shell reef is always better fishing with the incoming tide, and vice versa with the outgoing tide. Fish tend to favor one gut at one end of the reef with the incoming tide, and another gut at the opposite end of a shell reef with the outgoing tide.

Hanna's Reef in East Galveston Bay, Shell Island in West Galveston Bay, Bird Island in East Matagorda Bay, Panther Reef in San Antonio Bay, plus many others along the coast have been big producers for me over the years. I've caught thousands and thousands of trout and redfish on these reefs, especially on cold, dark, rainy, windy nights.

Always approach an exposed shell reef—or any shell reef— as quietly as possible. Never anchor your boat on the reef, and never walk on top of the reef. The scraping of your boat bottom and the grinding sound of your feet carry a *long* way underwater. These sounds spook game fish and disturb the entire fishing area. Don't do it.

Instead, anchor your boat away from and behind the reef (on the calm side of the reef) and drop into the water. Position yourself near the end of the reef in waist-deep water. Don't move around or shuffle your feet; this scares bait as well as game fish away. Cast out, and let your lure float over the backbone near the end of the reef and into the deeper dropoff. Stay put, even if the fish aren't hitting when you get there. Do this for a half hour or so. Then if they're still not hitting, rest for an hour and come back and try again. Do this until the fish hit the reef and start to feed. When they do, they'll start hitting. I guarantee it. And when they start hitting, you'll have more action than you can handle.

When you're fishing a *submerged* reef, or one with only a small exposed area—Shell Island in West Galveston Bay, for example—position yourself in deeper water, a good casting distance away from the end of the exposed backbone. Cast your lure toward the shallow part of the backbone on the incoming tide side of the reef, and let your lure float over the submerged reef. Since most of the reef will be underwater, fish will be moving over the reef and feeding along its top as well as its sides.

Once the tide is in, work your way very slowly and quietly up and down the submerged reef. Most fish don't like to leave a good feeding area, and game fish love to feed around shell reefs. Schools of mullet and small baitfish will cover these reefs and the shallows around them—all natural attractions for feeding game fish.

My favorite places to wade fish are exposed oyster reefs out in the middle of the bay. The fish are always on the windy side, so you cannot drift in. You must ease in quietly, and anchor away from the reef, then walk around and fish the reef parallel, almost down the reef. Do not make any noise with your feet.

Reef fishing is always best in the spring, when the specks are cutting teeth.

20

Reels for the Wade Fishermen

Reels during the 1930s were precision made by American manufacturers. Shakespeare Tackle Company had Sportscast, a small narrow spool reel. The South Bend Tackle Company also had a narrow spool reel, the South Bend 60. The two companies later merged. Another favorite among the early competition casters was the Langly, a small, free-spooler casting reel.

These early reels all retailed for around seven dollars each. They were simple to take down and maintain, and were ideal for casting. I bought them by the case and gave my used reels away to young fishermen whenever the opportunity presented itself. They also were the last of American-made reels. When Garcia reels from Sweden entered the market during the late 1940s, American manufacturers for some reason didn't respond. After Garcia got a foothold in the American market, they killed the American reel industry. By 1955, the Ambassadeur 5000 and 5000C had 90 percent of the American casting market. To this day American reel manufacturers have never recovered. During the 1960s, Japan began manufacturing tackle and providing reels for saltwater lure fishermen. Today, the Japanese own the world's reel market, producing reels superior to the Swedish-made ones.

In the old days, you had to clean your reel after every saltwater fishing trip. Today, most of the new reels are made from lightweight, extremely durable products. Metal in these

The Shimano Pro Bantam reel was a favorite of the Plugger during the early 1980s. Photo by Joe Doggett, courtesy of the Houston Chronicle.

reels is noncorrosive (normally stainless steel). Many feature oversized brass gears, so your maintenance is kept to a minimum.

Always take the reel off your rod after each fishing trip into the Gulf. If the reel was not submerged in saltwater, just spray it with WD40, take it off the rod, and put it on the shelf. If submerged in saltwater, the reel must be disabled and cleaned.

If you'll do this after each fishing trip, your reels will last you a lifetime. Today I usually recommend five reels for wade fishermen: the Ambassadeur 4500C,B line capacity 135/14 lb.; gear ratio 5:1, Ambassadeur 5500C line capacity 135/14 lb.; gear ratio 4.7:1, the Garcia 5500 Deluxe Gold-Plated line capacity 100/14 lb.; the Shimano Bantam Mag line capacity 12/14 lb.; gear ratio 5:11, and the Quantum 600T.I. Low Profile line capacity 100/14 lb.

21

Fishing Rods for Wade Fishermen

Fishing rods were first made from bamboo, and fly rods were probably the first casting rods made. Early fly rods were from seven to ten feet long and were very light and sensitive. For me, the ideal flyrod is nine feet long.

Early salt water casting rods, however, were never over five feet long. The handle or grip was made to fit the palm of the hand for perfect control of the lure. I began tournament (competition) casting with these early rods with the Houston Angler's Club in 1938. We met at the Hermann Park Lake every Thursday night. Our top gun and champion was Kasmoraski, a Shakespeare Tackle representative. Other top casters were the late Earl Lingo of Houston, a custom rod maker and master of the trade; Charlie Chamberline; Bill Gramer; and a handful of others who liked to cast. These men were the professionals in the late 1930s. The club held casting tournaments and traveled to other cities to compete. The object was to cast a small, pear-shaped lure, and drop it on top of one (designated) of three small lily-pad-sized floating objects on the lake. These pads were placed at various distances from the shore. Your lure had to drop directly onto the pad, same as a wedge shot on the golf course. Some big money changed hands at these early competitions.

The Right Rod Length

During the 1930s, factory-made casting rods for wade fishermen were nonexistent. Virtually all the casting rods manufactured then were for fresh-water fishermen or the deep-blue water fishermen. So, we began making and experimenting with our own wade fishing rods.

The first ones we tried were about six feet long. The extra length came from a long, straight handle attached to a five-foot bamboo blank (bare rod). The longer handle made it easier to fight the larger, stronger saltwater fish by using the belt line and taking some pressure off the wrist. SiloFlex finally began manufacturing a single-piece fiberglass blank rod up to seven feet long. Lingo and another Houstonian, Zollie Taliaferro—both rod makers—designed and manufactured the first prototypes of these rods. Soon big manufacturers were copying and mass-producing the designs.

The seven-foot-fiberglass blank was an excellent length. It had perfect balance and was lightweight. Best of all, the handle for these new rods was manufactured as part of the blank itself.

So, what is the right length for wade fishing? Over the years I've experimented with all lengths of rods up to eight and one-half feet. Because of my casting technique. I settled finally on a six-foot, nine-inch graphite rod with a nine-inch straight handle. Overall, I believe, it's the ideal length for saltwater wade fishing—at least for me. The weight of the rod and reel is all in your hand—not in front to make your rod tip heavy. This makes the rod less tiresome when you wade or surf-fish for long hours, which I do. (All my casting rods were custom-made by Lingo, until his death in 1990.)

I've since field tested several factory-made graphite rods— all copies of Lingo's and Taliaferro's models.

Lew Childree introduced the hard, nonfriction, graphite guides and rod tips in the United States; in my opinion, the best on the market and a great advance for wade fishing rods.

After experimenting with all sizes and lengths, Plugger settled on a six-foot-nine-inch graphite rod with a nine-inch straight handle, still his favorite. Photo courtesy Joe Doggett and the Houston Chronicle.

As a wade fisherman, you'll be continually casting and retrieving your lure—all day or night, hour in, hour out—and sometimes you'll tire. But stay with it, and you'll soon find your casting arm will get stronger each time you fish.

If you're not sure what length you want, the best rod to start with is probably a six-foot, three-inch medium-action rod with a nine-inch handle to butt onto a belt line (for comfort when landing a twenty-pound fish). With a light reel—no more than sixteen ounces—this type of rod can be fished for hours without tiring you out. This length of rod also is ideal for both top-water and sinking lures, especially the one-quarter ounce size.

22

Lures for the Wade Fisherman

Single-hook lures are the way of the future. If they're ever outlawed, it will mean we're almost out of fish and it won't matter anyway. Alaska has single-hook laws on the books and in some areas even prohibits lures with barbed hooks. Texas and other Gulf states should consider similar laws.

As the limits on saltwater game fish become smaller, the need to release fish with as little injury as possible becomes paramount. There's less chance of permanently injuring the fish prior to release when he's taken on a single-hook lure. This isn't a problem among true sportsmen, most of whom already use single-hook lures.

The fact is you don't need six hooks on a lure to catch a fish. One hook will do the job, and there's an excellent variety of single-hook lures available—the Johnson Spoon and shrimp tails. These lures are as good fish-getters as you can find, and they do minimum harm to the fish.

During the course of a year, I'll guide anywhere between a hundred and three hundred fishermen in the Gulf. Always I recommend they use single-hook lures. On any given half-day fishing excursion in the Chandeleurs, I'll catch and release anywhere between twenty and fifty fish. With a single hook, the fish almost always hooks himself in the corner of his lip and is easily unhooked, virtually unharmed.

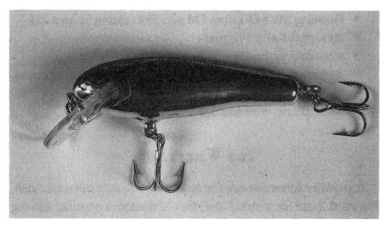

The Bagley Finger Mullet lure is used as a floater (if fast retrieved) or sinker (if worked beneath the surface). It is a good lure for most saltwater game fish.

Multiple- or treble-hook lures often hook the fish through the eye. I've caught them with these hooks hanging from their heads, jaws, throats, and eyes.

Treble-hook lures need to become collectors' items, and tackle manufacturers would do well to help them become so. Laws to outlaw multiple-hook lures are on the way.

And as today's metal and plastic lures get better, bait fishing may go the way of the treble hook.

Lures and Tackle Box Items

At a minimum, I recommend the following lures and items for your tackle box if you're going to wade fish:

- Several floater-type Plugger Bubble lures (assorted colors) or something similar (your choice)
- 1/4, 1/2, and 3/4 oz. Johnson Weedless Minnows (gold, copper, silver, and chartreuse)
- 1/4, 1/2, and 3/4 oz. Johnson Sprite Spoons (gold, silver, copper, and chartreuse)
- Several bucktails (white, pink, and yellow)
- Sinking Mirr-O-Lures 52M21, 52M28, 52M51 (colors 51 and 21)

Lures for the Wade Fisherman

- Floating Mirr-O-Lures 7M and 5M (colors 51 and 21)
- Assorted Kelly Wigglers
- Assorted jig heads
- Assorted Bagley Night Minnow or Finger Mullet Lures
- #12 and #14 swivels (no snap-ons)
- 58 lb. piano wire (for leaders)

Top-Water Lures

Top-water lures are my favorite way to catch saltwater fish. I've used them for years. Now, they've become popular among saltwater lure purists. Catching fish on top-water lures requires skill and patience. The lure has to be kept alive with small movement. Never reel a top-water plug in continuously. Allow the lure to stop for a split second, but don't give a fish time to examine the lure. Make two or three quick turns on the handle, and start it again. If a fish is nearby, he'll hit the lure while it's trying to "get away." Again, don't let him examine the lure. Let it stay only for a split second, then take the lure away. The strike will come when the lure is getting away.

People often think saltwater fish can't catch a fast-moving lure. Not true. Reds, mackerel, and bluefish are explosive over short distances and can catch anything you reel, no matter how fast. The trick is to keep it moving so fish can't examine it. In fact, it's impossible to reel a lure—float or sinker—too fast, even with the 5-to-1 ratio reels. The fish is quicker than your eye, and there's no way to take it away.

For top-water lure fishing, I recommend a Plugger Bubble type lure, or "broken-back" top-water plugs like the Cotton Cordell Redfin, the Bomber Long A, the Rapala Jointed Floating Minnow, Heddon's Torpedos, and the Zara Spook.

Sinking Lures

A plastic shrimp tail on about a sixteen-inch leader behind a Plugger Bubble is a good sinking lure combination.

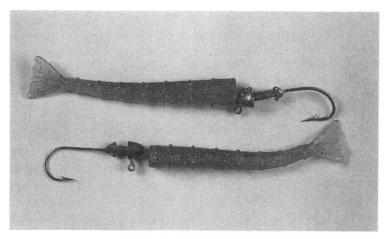

A Kelly Wiggler rigged with a one-quarter-ounce lead head jig tied with piano wire. Trailed a few inches behind a Plugger Bubble type floating lure, this rig is dynamite on specks and reds.

A sinking lure—used in water three feet or deeper—does not require as much skill as a top-water lure, but it does require a natural action. Again, never reel your lure in a straight line or continuously. All fish—bait or otherwise—accelerate with their tails and move through the water erratically in short lopes. Natural food like shrimp swim with a lope, accelerating much like jellyfish. To mimic this lope, push down then pull up on your reel handle. By doing this, you put a lope movement on the tip of your rod. The lure lopes up and down beneath the surface, much like a live shrimp.

Also, I use a Plugger Bubble type lure in water about three feet with a shrimp tail trailed about twenty-four inches below the bubble—fished slow with a tight line ready to set the hook. I also recommend gold, silver, or chartreuse Johnson Spoons as sinking lures for deeper water.

One of five ways to rig a Plugger Bubble type lure. Here a weedless bass hook is covered with a plastic Hawaiian skirt. It's a 100 percent weedless lure that's ideal for shallow, grassy flats.

Lures for Grassy Flats and Shallow Water

Shallow, grassy flats are only productive during the summer months and you have to know how to fish them or you'll wind up frustrated.

Bear in mind it's virtually impossible to pull a clean lure through grassy flats. So, the trick is to fish on top of the water and grass, especially during midday when the overhead sun pulls the grass upward toward the top of the water.

The best lures to use when fishing a grassy flat—especially in shallow water of three feet or less—are the floating Plugger Bubble type lures and the Johnson Weedless Spoons fished with a bucktail or dry rind. I developed the Plugger Bubble specifically for this type of fishing. It was the first, and I think the only, saltwater lure ever made that allows you to fish very shallow water, grassy flats, and shell reefs slowly without getting grassed or hung up.

I fish the Plugger Bubble with a small Johnson Weedless Spoon attached to a pink or yellow bucktail, trailing about eighteen inches behind. The bubble keeps your lure up and out

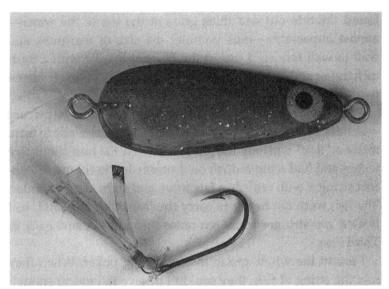

Plugger Bubble rigged with a single hook and bucktail. This combination works for specks and reds in both deep and shallow water.

of the grass. Yet, it still looks good enough for game fish to hit—which they do and which, by the way, is why I put a hook in it.

The hook trails easily behind the Plugger Bubble. A twist tail or a small Johnson Sprite Spoon in a bucktail looks good to fish, too. I've caught—and have watched others catch—doubles on this combination.

Stan Slaten discovered the Plugger Bubble on a fishing trip we made to the Laguna's Third Pass. The wind was from the south, the surf was muddy, and the water going through the Third and Fourth Passes had muddied the whole lagoon. When we flew in, I spotted green water in a large grassy flat—about forty acres—roughly five miles north of where our camp would be. Everything else looked like chocolate milk. Since I'd fished the pass before, I knew the fish would be in the grass.

Everyone decided it was too muddy to fish and started a card game. I took a couple of Johnson Spoons and Plugger Bubbles, left the group, and headed for the grass. It was about five miles over sand dunes and weeds to the lagoon. When I got there, I found the tide out and thick grass at the top of the water—almost impassable—plus potholes the size of washtubs and wall-to-wall redfish. I rigged the Plugger Bubble with a four-inch trailer and a small, single short-shank, No. 1 hook between two white bucktails—one on each side of the barb.

I knew the bubble would float and would be about 90 percent weedless. I cast it in front of some redfish, waited for one to turn, made a "tick" with my rod tip that moved the lure about five inches and had a big redfish on. I proceeded to fill my fifteen-foot stringer with redfish, a few trout, and eight large flounder. The fish were too heavy to carry the five miles overland, so I floated my stringer some ten miles through the surf back to Third Pass.

I found the whole group inside playing poker. When they saw the string of fish, they couldn't believe it. I found enough Plugger Bubbles for everyone in the party and we spent the next two days air boating back to the grassy flats, catching over two hundred fish. The bubble saved the trip, and I knew then it was a commercially sound lure.

When Slaten got back to Houston, he announced and promoted the Plugger Bubble on his TV show. Bob Brister also picked up on the bubble's use in the *Houston Chronicle*. The bubble eventually became known among wade fishermen in Texas, Louisiana, and Mississippi.

The Plugger Bubble is no longer made, but there still are a few of them tucked in tackle boxes around the Gulf.

Spoon Lures

If I were stranded on an island with a rod and reel and someone told me I could have only one lure with which to catch fish and feed myself, I would ask for a Johnson Spoon.

My two favorites are the Johnson Silver Minnow and the Johnson Sprite.

The spoon—sometimes called the Silver Minnow—originated with Louis Johnson in Chicago during the 1920s. Johnson was

The Silver Minnow (left), first introduced in 1920. The Silver Minnow Sprite (right), first introduced in 1950. Reprinted with permission, courtesy of Johnson Lures.

a retired Chicago foundry operator who liked to fish. He began by cutting handles off tablespoons and soldering hooks onto their interiors. But the spoons gave him trouble in weeds, so he developed a guard to ward off weeds and protect the hook (spawning the term weedless).

It worked so well fishermen started asking for them, and Johnson began casting and selling his famous "Silver Spoon." It became the flagship lure for the Louis Johnson Company—Johnson Lures—during the 1930s. During the Depression, the company introduced the small Johnson Sprite, the Lujon, and the Bucktail Spoon lures—all excellent redfish and speckled trout lures to this day.

The weedless, single-hook Johnson Spoons, fished fast to keep it off bottom in grassy flats and with a pair of bucktails to hide the barb, are excellent fish-getters.

I recommend the silver, gold, copper, and chartreuse one-quarter-ounce No. 73142 Johnson Spoon. (When fishing the surf, use a three-quarter ounce 73306 Gold Johnson Sprite Spoon, equipped with a short wire leader. Fish stay on the bottom in the surf, and you're always casting into the wind—hence the need for the heavier lure.)

Always fish your Johnson Spoon with a teaser or plastic bucktail. Attach the bucktail to the split ring along with the hook. It will draw fish to the hook and not the spoon. Also, remember to replace any treble hooks with a No. 1 stainless-steel Eagle Claw® hook. When fishing a heavy grassy flat with

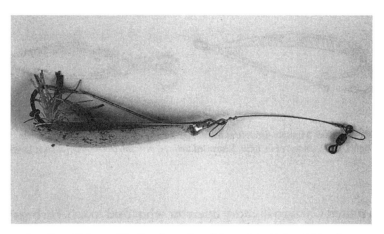

A well-used Johnson Weedless Spoon from Plugger's tackle box. Note wire leader and swivel.

a spoon, attach two bucktails—one on either side of the hook—to make your spoon virtually weedproof or "weedless."

Never use a split ring in front of your lure. This adds weight to your spoon and catches grass. Simply make a twist ring using No. 58 pound, stainless-steel piano wire. Tie directly into the nose with the wire and then onto a small No. 14 swivel about three inches away.

If you rig your spoon this way, it will outlast its finish, even when you're into schools of sharp-tooth blues and snook.

Drift Fishing Lures

When fishing water deeper than four feet, I recommend drift fishing. It's ideal for older people, children, or anyone unable to wade but who enjoys fishing and being outdoors. Drift fishermen were another reason I developed the Plugger Bubble. Just cast the bubble out, pull out some line, let it go behind the boat, and hold on. Wave action does all the work and puts the necessary moves on the lure to attract fish. It's an exciting way to drift fish.

The Plugger Bubble rigged with a one-quarter-ounce leadhead jig and Kelly Shrimp Tail that trails about twenty to twenty-five inches behind. This combination is an excellent drift-fishing lure.

I also recommend the shrimp tail with a one-eighth-ounce lead head tied several inches under a Plugger Bubble type lure or popping cork.

Deep-Running Lures

During hot summer months when temperatures hit ninety degrees or above, fish move to the bottom where the water is cooler and deeper. The only way to take them is on deep-running lures. Put your floaters back in your box, and use deep-running lures. The lead-headed shrimp tail jig is my favorite. Kelly Wigglers (Alpha Bait Company) makes an excellent shrimp tail. I tie directly to the jig head and fish deep with a "lope" action to resemble a live shrimp. Keep a tight line at all times and be ready to set the hook with the slightest touch or hint of a hit.

Lures for the Wade Fisherman

An old Plugger Bubble rigged with a No. 4 steel-shank hood and small spinner. The lure works best with teaser or bucktail covering the hook. It was used for either small saltwater or fresh-water gamefish. Today Plugger recommends a single hook instead of the treble.

A Plugger Bubble type lure with a shrimp tail trailed about twenty-four inches below the bubble—fished slow with a tight line ready to set the hook when you feel the bump—will work in three to four feet of water. In deeper water I recommend gold, silver, or chartreuse Johnson Spoons.

Be certain not to stand erect in your boat while drift fishing. The fish can see you from a long distance and will not be attracted by your lure. Stay down low.

Surf-Fishing Lures

The best lures to use for surf-fishing are also deep-running lures. Use something that will run close to the bottom like a three-quarter-ounce Johnson Sprite Spoon, either silver or gold. A plastic shrimp tail with a three-quarter-ounce head and white bucktail, or a silver or gold Tony Accetta Spoon (1 1/4 oz.), will also work.

If you cast your lure across or in front of the tide in the gut, it will settle fast and wash back up on the beach. The trick is to cast your lure upstream in the gut parallel to the shore, let it settle to the bottom, then let the tide do the work for you. Just keep your line tight and move down with the tide. Often you won't even have to retrieve.

Night Fishing

The best lures to use for night fishing are solid white floaters. Stay a good casting distance away from the reef, and let your lure float over the top in shallow water with the baitfish.

Shell Reef Lures

When fishing deeper water at the end of a long reef, try a one-quarter-ounce silver or gold spoon with a bucktail. When fishing water two feet or less on top of the reef, use a white floating plug or a Plugger Bubble type lure with a plastic shrimp tail trailing. The bubble is good day or night in these shallower situations.

When working the top of a wide reef, which might be several hundred yards wide and a mile long, use a good top-water lure like the Plugger Bubble or the Cardill Shifting Shiner hooked through the nose.

Mirr-O-Lure makes the 7M floater, another good lure for shell reefs. The 7M floater is an easy lure to fish—especially for beginners—and virtually anyone can get enough distance on it to reach fish. Most successful wade fishermen carry Plugger Bubble type lures, Johnson Spoons, a few Mirr-O-Lures and an assortment of Kelly Wigglers and shrimp tails.

I used to use either a Cardill Shifting Shiner or the Mirr-O-Lure 7M floater, but now I use a floating bubble with a quarter-ounce Johnson Spoon trailing behind about eight to twelve inches.

23

How to Wade Fish a Saltwater Lure

With the right lure you can catch any saltwater game fish within casting distance, even if the fish isn't hungry. All you have to do is to put the lure in front of—or around—the fish where he can see it. Next, apply the right action to make your lure imitate something alive or edible, or both.

How your lure is retrieved is also important. For example, most wade fishermen try to fish too fast for trout and redfish in deep water and not fast enough in shallow water. One of the best things that ever happened for shallow-water wade fishing was the 5-to-1 fast retrieve reel.

The action of the lure must be controlled by the person behind it. This is true whether you're wade fishing, drift fishing, shallow or grassy-flat fishing, shore fishing, deep-water fishing, or surf-fishing.

Cast your lure overhead (not sidearm) straight over the top—fast—and let the whip of your rod tip do the work. Use a smooth follow-through, much like a golf swing. Done right, there's virtually no strain or effort on your arm.

There are two basics you must remember to make a good clean cast. First, thumb your reel lightly the entire time your lure is in flight. Watch your lure as it approaches the water. The moment it makes contact with the water, apply your second basic: stop the reel instantly and completely with your thumb. That's the secret to successful casting—otherwise you get backlash.

I hold my rod almost vertically when retrieving and "lope" my lure in by reeling like I'm cranking a freezer full of home-made ice cream. Push down, pull up. Push down, pull up. Not too fast, not too slow. Work on it. The retrieve came naturally to me. I found the retrieve automatically makes the tip of my rod move up and down. This movement at my rod tip makes the lure "lope" or appear alive and active at all times. The lope works especially well when you're fishing knee-deep water. In shallower water or flats, keep the lure higher on the surface (and off the bottom) by reeling it in faster.

You'll find, though, no matter which way you work a lure, you'll get results if you're near saltwater game fish.

Remember, too, that most saltwater game fish are virtually faster than the eye. They'll come out of nowhere to hit your lure, usually near a pothole where they're hiding or in grass where they're waiting for something to cross an open spot.

When you fish a wide gut, wade the edge and cast your lure across it. Fan your casts in all directions. Slow your lure down. Let it hit and drop into the gut, then bring it in fast. You'll find good action this way around guts.

Experience is always your best teacher. Remember the type of situation you were in, what you did, and where you were each time they hit your lure. You'll be thinking like saltwater game fish before long.

When I first started fishing the shallow flats around Port O'Connor, Port Mansfield, and Mexico's Laguna Madre, for example, I had to fish my lures fast to keep them out of the grass. This wasn't a real problem where redfish were concerned be-cause they're quick and fast and strong and can hit a spoon six to eight feet away so fast you can't follow the movement. Specks and flounder, on the other hand, aren't that quick. I noticed I often zipped lures past them too fast to hit while trying to keep them out of the grass.

Consequently, I learned to either slow down or speed my lure up, depending on the situation and the type of fish I was after.

24

Color and Fish

Fish are not color-blind. They can see clearly on the darkest nights and distinguish colors.

Saltwater fish living where the water is very clear are silver or bluish. This makes them almost invisible and lets them blend with the clear water background. When these fish move into the bays to spawn, they change their colors and become brownish, staying that way until they return to clear water, where they change back to bright silver or bluish.

The reason for this change is obvious. The color change acts as a camouflage to protect them from predator fish. If fish were color-blind, coloring wouldn't matter.

The color of a lure has everything to do with catching saltwater fish. I've fished on days knowing *exactly* where the fish were, but could not get them to strike a certain color lure. A fishing partner standing next to me would be casting the identical lure—only a different color—into the same school of fish and he would have one on every cast. I've lost track of the number of times I've seen this happen. I've experimented with color many times and always end up with the same results. Redfish, specks, Spanish mackerel—the only difference would be the color of my lure. The fish would hit one color, but not another.

One winter day my partner and I were fishing in Offat's Bayou. We were both casting green, No. 18, silver-side 52M Mirr-O-Lures and not getting a strike. Another fisherman—not

The Johnson Sprite Spoon rigged with a leader wire and swivel, a teaser, and a preferable single hook, is the "best all-around saltwater lure available," according to the Plugger.

a hundred feet away—was catching speckled trout every cast. We were all casting on top of the same reef. He was using a Mirr-O-Lure, 52M28, red with gold sides. When my partner and I switched to his color of lure, the action was wall to wall. These fish *wanted* something red and would not touch a green lure that day, though I'd seen the green lure catch fish exactly like our red lures, only in other locations and at a different time.

On another occasion in Copano Bay near Rockport, Bill Gramer and I were anchored near the end of Long Reef, casting Johnson Silver Spoons alongside a small stick we'd stuck in the reef to mark the drop-off. I caught twenty speckled trout on a silver spoon with a red bucktail. Gramer was casting a silver spoon with a yellow bucktail and did not get a strike. Gramer was noted for his stubbornness, but that day he changed to a red bucktail and had a fish on every cast. I've seen many days when the fish would only strike a white lure. Other days they would hit a black and silver combination.

Color and Fish

During the late 1930s, there were very few colors available other than those found on homemade lures that a few other purists and I made. When I first started saltwater plugging during the 1930s, I whittled hundreds of lures from mahogany and painted them with white pearl nail polish. Most of these were floaters even though I made a few sinkers. I tied them all in the nose—another first—and found the solid white lure to be the number one attraction for saltwater game fish at the time. Doug English and Pluggin' Shorty out of Corpus Christi did the same, and the white saltwater lure became famous among early Gulf wade fishermen. We continued experimenting with colors and began to find that fish hit different colors at different times.

I have at least three tackle boxes of lures of almost every color made. Some are old and would be considered collectors' items, but I still use them because they catch fish.

Fishing Colors

In general, I recommend the following colors. However, if you're on fish and they're not hitting your color, try another until you find one they turn on to. Fish will surprise you. They're not dumb.

Conditions	Recommended Colors
Bright sunshine, clear water	White, silver, or gold
Daytime, overcast or light drizzle	Bright colors, red, green, strawberry
Amber or green water	Chartreuse
Daytime, wind, rain, storm (sandy) waters	Fluorescent lures or yellow redheads
Clear nights, calm water	Solid white, mullet colors
Cloudy nights, storm waters	Solid white, silver
Murky water	Yellow redheads or fluorescent lures
Very muddy water	Wait for it to clear (Don't waste your time)

25

The Right Fishing Line

Your "fishing line" should be strong enough to match your
tackle. I recommend no less than a fourteen-pound monofilament line for the average wade fisherman. For beginners, I
recommend seventeen-pound monofilament line to keep the
fish from breaking off with the lure and several feet of trailing
line. My reels are equipped with fourteen-pound, soft, flexible
monofilament line like Courtland's PLION II or Triline Line.
There is other good line on the market, too. Just remember:
Saltwater fishing requires long-distance casting and a softer line
will give you more distance. Lines like the ones mentioned give
me the necessary casting distance but do not recoil like a hard
line. Consequently, it prevents any "professional overruns"
(backlashes). I keep one reel loaded with seventeen-pound
monofilament line for night fishing, which gives me a little extra
to horse the fish in.

So, use *enough* line. A fish that breaks away has to spend the
rest of his life dragging his line with the lure in his mouth or
jaw. I've lost count of the number of fish I've landed with old
treble hooks either embedded in their jaws, hanging onto the
side of their heads, or under their throats.

Today, fishing line and a good, strong, single hook are two
of the cheapest, yet most important, parts of your tackle.

New technology now allows manufacturers to make line
thinner and stronger, too. A fourteen-pound test line is the same

size as a ten-pound test used to be. Consequently, most good wade fishing reels will hold more than a hundred yards of line.

Plus, the new "mono" line has a stretch to it that acts as a shock cushion once a fish peels out forty or fifty yards. When this happens, the line almost doubles in strength. The closer you bring the fish in toward you, the more the line returns toward its original test.

When fishing the surf from shore, let the fish have a bunch of line on the first run then set your drag or thumb the spool and let him wallow for a few seconds. At forty or fifty yards or more it's almost impossible to break this new line.

If you hook a big fish on light tackle, keep the pressure on the fish tight and don't try to reel a large fish—tarpon, jack fish, bull red—in all at once. Rather, taking up a little slack, walk backwards until you beach a large fish.

This technique will save you time, plus you do not have to spook your fish in the water while trying to land it, which occasionally leads to a broken line and lost tackle.

26

Use Good *Single* Hooks

Alaska and Canada already have single-hook laws that even prohibit barbs on hooks. When I began fishing with artificial lures at age eight, most of the first lures I created had multiple hooks. Later in my career I found I could catch just as many or more fish on a simple lure with a single hook.

I would like to see the United States go to this concept. I've seen what treble hooks do to fish—they imbed in the eyes, gills, and side of the head—only a small portion of treble-hooked fish survive. Many are blinded in at least one eye, and many have their throats ripped from the treble hook when released.

Fish can be easily and cleanly caught on single hooks, and under our catch-and-release program, most will survive when released.

I recommend the forged Eagle Claw® 1/0 single- or double-snelled hook—either bronze or gold-plated—with a plain shank offset. Of the two, the gold-plated hook lasts longer in salt water.

Stainless-steel, nickel, or cadmium-plated hooks also last well in salt water, if you can find them to purchase.

I like Eagle Claw® hooks because they will hold 80 percent of all strikes. There are other good hooks on the market. In my experience, cheap hooks will only hold about 50 percent of all your strikes when you're wade fishing.

1/0
FORGED

Eagle Claw® hook. Illustration courtesy of Eagle Claw® Fishing Tackle.

27

One Knot Ties Your Lures

There are as many ways to tie knots onto leaders as there are kinds of leaders and leader material. In fact, most fishing tackle exhibitions feature a fishing line manufacturer's expert showing several ways to tie on a lure. It makes for an interesting show and good conversation and is usually educational.

I've experimented with all kinds of ways to tie a good leader knot over the years, and I've settled on the double clinch knot. It is, in my opinion, the best knot—both the strongest and smallest—for tying onto your lure.

With the new monolines being softer, thinner, and stronger, the double clinch knot is your best knot. It's strong, only requires about three inches of line, will not slip or break, and does not require any trimming. You can even leave the surplus line to act as a weed guard.

You tie the double the same way as your regular clinch knot but don't stop. Thread the end of the line through the eye and back through your loop once more, (for your "double") then tighten.

How to Tie a Double Clinch Knot

The double clinch knot is the best way to attach monofilament to a lure, swivel, or hook. To make the knot:

1. Put the line through the eye.
2. Make three to five turns around the standing line, but don't tighten.
3. Thread line through the loop above the eye, then back through the large loop. DO THIS TWICE.

Double clinch knot. Courtesy of Stren Fishing Lines.

4. Pull coils tight against the eye so they don't overlap. Trim.

Double clinch knot. Courtesy of Stren Fishing Lines.

5. The knot will not come undone.

28

Bucktails and Dry Rinds Catch Fish, Too

In the early years we fished with original bucktails made from real deer hair, hence, the name. Today's version—still called a "bucktail"—is made from plastic. The plastic is better, lighter, and comes in multiple colors.

Bucktails—also called "teasers"—are the best way to conceal a hook and play a major role in catching fish on artificial lures, especially spoons. Any game fish will hit the last thing trailing. Don't ever fish a spoon without one. The lighter colors tend to resemble fish and are especially useful on jigs.

Pork rinds were used during the early days to dress up the spoons, too. This practice has evolved to today's dry rind. The dry rind is made from real deer skin and when wet, becomes soft and wiggles like pork rind. Dry rinds are available in multicolors and can be cut in small V patterns and attached to the ring of the spoon along with the hook. The dry rind stays soft, and its movement through water attracts fish. Dry rinds are especially effective on weedless spoons and help keep other lures weedless, as well.

Keep a good supply of both bucktails and dry rinds in your tackle box and use them with single hooks.

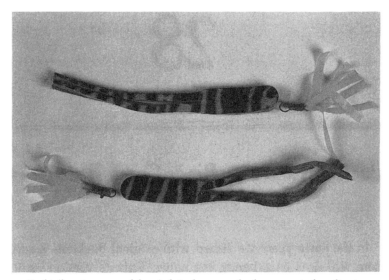

Bucktailers, teasers, and dry rinds to dress your hooks are musts for saltwater wade fishermen.

29

Use the Right Leader and Swivel

One morning in the Chandeleur Islands I cast into a large school of blues (runners) in the surf using a Mirr-O-Lure without a wire leader. A large blue bit it off. I worked my way half a mile down the beach, hooked the same blue again, and retrieved my lure. In this case it wasn't the fault of the line. Blues have sharp teeth and can bite through heavy monofilament leaders. (In fact, fish like blues and tarpon can clean out your tackle box in no time.) It was situations like this one that led me over the years to my short-wire leaders. Now, it's standard equipment for me. In fact, *every* lure in my tackle box has a short-wire leader on it. They save me hundreds of lures a year.

Leaders play an important part in rigging saltwater lures. Speckled trout, redfish, Spanish mackerel, snook, ladyfish, bluefish, sheepshead, flounder—all have sharp teeth or very coarse mouths. Leaders for these fish, therefore, should be made with a small-diameter stainless wire—not over sixty-pound test and never over two to three inches in length—twisted simultaneously with the lure to ensure an even twist on the wire. Leave a small loop at the attachment so the line will work fully, and put a small swivel at the other end of the leader. The leader will be just long enough for the fish's mouth. *Attach these leaders permanently to each of your lures in your spare time* so you'll always be ready to go wade fishing. It will save you from having to buy new lures each time out.

Because every good lure is balanced and designed to perform a certain way, any additional weight—such as a wire leader too big, long, or heavy—will kill the action. Leaders that are too long, for example, will kink and make the lure malfunction.

The short, two- to three-inch wire leader with the very small swivel will keep the lure from twisting your line and will make your lure cast better and perform as expected. *Never* use any type of a snap-on. Twist your leader wire directly into the nose of the lure and use the double cinch knot to tie your small swivel onto your line. A small size No. 14 swivel is strong enough to land a forty- to fifty-pound fish. Plus, it's small enough to thread through the eye on your rod without damaging the tip.

30

Wade Fishing Equipment and Clothing

If you've wired and tied your lures, leaders, and line properly, you don't need to lug a lot of stuff into the water with you. Some extra lures, a candy bar, and a pocketknife will do. When I wade fish, I fish. I travel far, fast, and light unless I'm working the end of a reef or a night spot like the drop-off at Bird Island. I always carry a few spare lures in a plastic box or a heavy-duty plastic bag tucked inside my shirt pocket. If I'm going where the action will be fast, I may carry an extra reel with me.

But what you use in the water is up to you. If you plan on wading great distances during summer months, wear a light, cool cap or hat; jeans; high-top tennis shoes; a light, long-sleeved cotton shirt; and a fifteen- or twenty-foot stringer.

I keep my extra gear in my tackle box (get a good, large one) in my boat. When I need it, I wade over there and get it. Otherwise, the only thing I pull through the water with me is my stringer of fish. Besides regular tackle, I keep a few things in my boat like needle-nose pliers (regular hardware type), some Adolph's meat tenderizer (in case of a stingray hit), sunglasses, a sharp filleting knife, waterproof matches, containers, chests to ice my fish, a flashlight, life vests, and a good first aid kit.

You'll need good foul-weather gear for fishing cold, rainy, windy winter nights and days. I recommend insulated long underwear (top and bottom) and socks, especially if you're going to be in cold water for several hours. You'll also need good waders. I've always used GRA-LITE's all-weather boot-foot chest waders with straps, but there are other manufacturers with comparable products. I always found the GRA-LITE waders warm and comfortable, easy to get in and out of. Plus, they're double-sewn and sealed to guard against leaks.

The GRA-LITE parka is an excellent cold-weather parka for damp, windy winter weather or for use during a cold storm. The parka, like the wader, is mildew resistant, double-sewn and sealed. The parka has big pockets and reinforced zippers, and is loose and comfortable.

Recommended Equipment and Clothing

Here's a handy packing list for your wade fishing trips:

Belt with attachments to hold lures
Cold-weather gear
Current license with saltwater stamp, personal
    identification
Extra batteries (flashlight as well as a spare boat battery)
Extra clothes
Extra reel
Extra rod
Flashlight
Fully-stocked tackle box
Insect spray
Landing net
Life vests (when wading deeper water—especially at
    night—and always for boating)
Needle-nose pliers
Rain gear
Sun lotion
Sunglasses
Tennis shoes
Waders

31

My Million Pounds of Fish

For the last fifty years I've fished, on the average, at least every other day (or night). I can't remember a time when I didn't fill my stringer with fifteen or twenty fish and release at least fifty more if I was into some hot action. Before I started fishing the Gulf, I caught hundreds of bass. I've also waded, on average, at least two to five miles each time I went out. I'd guess I've waded close to 4,000 miles of Gulf water in my lifetime. This ought to be some kind of record, too!

The major groups of fish I've caught are bluefish, tarpon, Spanish mackerel, snook, ladyfish, redfish and speckled trout.

Bluefish

I've probably caught more bluefish than anything else. During the 1940s and 1950s, bluefish were wall to wall in the surf close to San Luis Pass and around the boulders.

You won't find them in abundance like that anymore, but they're still in the Gulf. Bluefish are edible and considered a delicacy on the East Coast where they grow much larger than in the Gulf.

Gulf blues are seldom over five pounds. They're always near the shore in the first gut and can be caught from shore. You'll

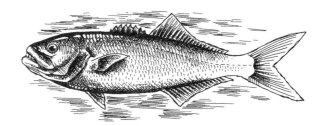

Bluefish. Artwork courtesy of Texas Parks and Wildlife Graphics Department.

also find them in the surf during the summer months. Sometimes they'll keep specks and redfish away from your lure. I've seen fifteen to twenty blues fight over a lure. They're fun to catch and will go airborne for several jumps when they're hooked. They're a real game fish for any sports fisherman looking for hot action. They're also a popular fly rod fish, as well.

Take care when unhooking your bluefish. They have strong teeth and are capable of biting the end of your finger. You can unhook a blue by stepping lightly on its head and removing your hook.

Several times I've removed the hook from my lure and cast into a school of blues to watch them fight for it. After forty-five minutes or so, the lure looks like it was dragged down an interstate behind a truck!

Tarpon

The tarpon has been glamorized, glorified, and publicized over the years. Consequently, sportsmen travel hundreds of miles to fish for tarpon. Florida is the most popular location for tarpon. Fly-fishing for tarpon also has become popular. Personally, I wouldn't drive across the street to catch one.

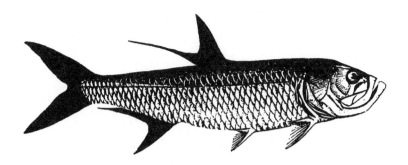

Tarpon. Artwork courtesy of Texas Parks and Wildlife Graphics Department.

During the first half of the century, tarpon were abundant along the Gulf Coast into Mexico. I've caught and released hundreds of them in Texas passes and rivers and in Mexico during the 1940s and 1950s, most were small, ranging from ten to twenty pounds. In fact, the mouth of the Brazos River at Freeport once was the tarpon capital of Texas. Now, the tarpon is almost extinct in Texas waters. Pollution killed them. I also witnessed the dynamiting of millions of fish—mainly tarpon—up the Soto la Marina River in Mexico during the 1940s. The fish were used for fertilizer. Snook, specks, and reds were sacrificed along with them. It was a slaughter.

I like to eat whatever I catch, and if I can't eat it, I don't want to catch it. This is why I've always considered the tarpon a nuisance fish. Tarpon, a game fish, have no food value and about all they're good for, as far as I can tell, is to tear your tackle up. I've had tarpon clean out my tackle and spring several good reels.

When I fished Eighth Pass in Mexico during the 1940s and 1950s, I caught thousands of small tarpon, usually in the six- to twelve-pound range. I always released them. Tarpon always were present with the snook—which was why I fished Eighth Pass. If I never hook another tarpon, I won't be disappointed.

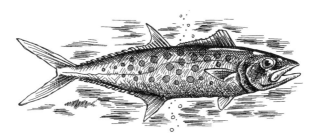

Spanish mackerel. Artwork courtesy of Texas Parks and Wildlife Graphics Department.

Spanish Mackerel

I've yet to walk away from a school of Spanish mackerel in more than fifty years of Gulf fishing. They're a scrappy, fun-to-catch game fish that cover the entire Gulf.

Spanish mackerel outnumber speckled trout in the Gulf about a thousand to one. I don't think they'll ever be an endangered species. When fully matured, the average mackerel reaches about thirty inches. Out in the Gulf they're bigger. They're strong and fast and will strike a lure when it's retrieved quickly. Trolling is the most effective way to catch mackerel. The best lures are silver spoons or small white jigs. Of the two, the white jig is most effective.

Spanish mackerel spawn several times a year, and it's almost impossible to land one without eggs. The fish is edible and can be fried or broiled. (They're delicious broiled in butter.) Marinate mackerel in vegetable oil and vinegar for at least thirty minutes before cooking. They're also delicious when smoked or pickled.

Snook. Artwork courtesy of Texas Parks and Wildlife Graphics Department.

Snook

The snook fights every bit as hard as the tarpon. He's a great game fish and—in my opinion—is one of the two best-eating fish in the world. In fact, the only other fish I'd rather eat is the red snapper. Nothing compares to snapper and snook. I caught thousands in Mexico during the 1940s and 1950s. Everything eighteen pounds or under I released, anything over I iced until my chests were full. Sometimes I'd fish and release hundreds over a two-day period after my chests were full.

Ladyfish

Ladyfish—also called the horse mackerel—are another nuisance fish. They have zero food value and are almost too plentiful. Few people keep them, even though they're caught all over the Gulf and bays.

Ladyfish are fun to catch if you're just looking for action, especially for beginners and kids. They're the next best fighters to bonefish (and even resemble them). You can hook one on a long cast; and before you can set the hook, he's already behind you. Ladyfish are very fast and aggressive, reach about four pounds, have a mouth like a snook, and can cut your lure off with ease.

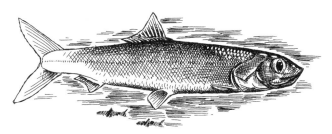

Ladyfish. Artwork courtesy of Texas Parks and Wildlife Graphics Department.

I recommend steel leaders. They'll strike anything moving, and I've yet to find a lure the ladyfish will pass up. You'll find them in the surf in large schools during the summer months.

I've caught and released tens of thousands of them over the years. On my first saltwater fishing trip to Turtle Bayou in Rockport during the late 1930s, I released over a hundred ladyfish. I also kept sixty big specks and reds that day.

Redfish and Speckled Trout

Redfish and speckled trout are my favorite species to catch. I place the speck and red in an elite class I call "choice eating fish" from the Gulf. Only the snook and snapper are better. I've eaten some type of fish at least three times a week all my life, and I've yet to lose my appetite for the choice fish.

I became hooked on redfish and speckled trout during the late 1930s. The fish were wall to wall in the Gulf through the 1950s, and our original group of saltwater lure fishermen caught thousands of them. We never kept a speck under eighteen inches or three pounds, and we never finished an overnight trip without filling our three-hundred pound iceboxes with gilled and gutted specks and reds. We probably released twice as many as we kept.

Red Drum (Redfish) and Spotted Sea Trout (Speckled Trout). Artwork courtesy of Texas Parks and Wildlife Graphics Department.

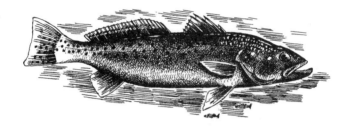

32

Caring for Your Catch

Fish meat—especially saltwater fish—is one of the healthiest, tenderest, and tastiest of all edible meats. It contains minerals essential to good health. Still, many people waste good fish by not knowing what to do after they catch a fish.

To me there's nothing quite like hooking a tough saltwater fish on an artificial lure. And whether you use a landing net or just play your fish to the finish—which I enjoy best—and wrestle him with your hands, it's all part of the thrill of catching a fish.

The next step is to string your fish right. When you're wade fishing, put the point of the fish stringer through both lips—not one lip—and not through the gills. Your fish has to breathe with his gills. Consequently, if his mouth cannot close completely (so he can breath through his gills), he'll drown within minutes in warm weather. When he does, the meat will spoil before you can get it on ice; or it will become soft and bloody and not fit for the table.

By stringing your fish through both lips, he'll stay alive for a longer period of time. This is especially true of redfish because they're tougher and can stand a lot of punishment. Remember, too, if you decide to release a red on your stringer, *he will not live if he's been on your stringer over an hour.* Speckled trout, on the other hand, are weak fish and will not survive a release once strung.

One of the worst practices is to catch a big stringer of fish then drag it over hot beach sand to your camp. Carry them high off the ground or, if your stringer is too heavy, walk through the surf and float it behind you.

My philosophy has always been, "If you catch it, eat it. And if you can't eat it, feed it to other creatures that can." So when filleting your fish, always put your scraps back into the water. There's a hungry creature there waiting. When I camp in the Chandeleurs, my favorite pastime is to cut my fish scraps into small pieces and feed them to the gulls, hardheads, croakers, and crabs around my houseboat.

I always let a member or two of my fishing party work on the filleting block with me. What's left over we cut up and feed to the birds, fish, and other creatures.

One of the most common mistakes fishermen make when caring for their catch is leaving the docks without sufficient ice. They carry one ice chest with less than twenty-five pounds of ice—usually cracked—to preserve their fish. Cracked ice lasts only a few hours and turns to water. The fish are placed in the water ungutted and gilled and left there all day, even overnight. All the while the meat is getting soft and spoiling.

That's why it's very important to take at least two ice chests with *block ice* in each one. To keep your fish fresh and the meat firm, clean your fish shortly after the catch. Do not remove the air bladder. If you leave it inside, the fish will remain firm and last much longer.

To clean your fish, cut the gills over and under, then pull *them with the insides in one jerk.* Rinse your fish. Next, lay him belly down on a layer of ice chipped from the block, then cover him with another layer of chipped ice. Go with a layer of ice, then a layer of fish, and so on. This method will keep your fish fresh for long periods of time.

During the late 1940s I fished for snook at Seventh and Eighth Passes in Mexico—a trip that required at least five to seven days. I always brought back at least five hundred pounds of filleted snook, averaging about twenty pounds each. The fish was kept fresh and firm using the method described above. I never lost a single fish.

Caring for Your Catch

After you fillet your fish, save the meat along the back—bone and "fish throats." They're ideal for seafood gumbo. Simply boil these bony pieces of fish for two to three minutes. Chill the mixture and use it as "lump crab meat" in soups, fish chowder, and gumbo.

Never put frozen fish into microwave ovens to thaw. Instead, place your frozen fish in clean, cold water and let it defrost naturally.

I still personally handle each day's catch on the cleaning table on my boat and fillet and eat virtually every fish I keep. And if I have more than I can eat, I always make sure other people get the meat.

Never waste your catch.

33

Preparing Your Fish and Game

Some kind of fish, shrimp, or oyster—anything that comes from unpolluted water—should be on everyone's diet at least three times a week.

Since the world is mostly covered by water, fish are available in every part of the world. Every unpolluted body of water is—at least for now—abundant with some kind of fish for the taking. Only the size and the limit are regulated.

And, almost every species is edible if prepared properly. Consequently, there's no need to specify speckled trout, redfish, or red snapper. There are other fish just as nutritious, just as tasty.

Proper seasoning and preparation of your catch or game is another key to good health. Seasoning is especially important when preparing fish, ducks, geese, quail, venison, or anything wild. My basic seasonings are salt, black pepper, tarragon, celery salt, cayenne pepper, vinegar, Italian herbs, paprika, and lots of fresh garlic.

When seasoning with garlic, *always* use real garlic mashed into a paste. Garlic not only adds flavor to food, but has medicinal qualities as well. It helps immunize the body from many common viruses and diseases such as colds, arthritis, and high blood pressure. I can't remember the last time I had a severe cold, and I'm in the water year round, winter included. Garlic

What better place than a houseboat's galley in the Chandeleurs to prepare a very tasty dish of fresh Spanish mackerel. Photo by Joe Doggett, courtesy of the Houston Chronicle.

also helps protect you from the effects of mosquitoes and other insect bites.

Here are some of my best fish and wild game recipes. Remember, one key to preparing good seafood is not to overcook it.

Seafood a la Chandeleur

(The Plugger's *original* recipe)

Serves 6

In a large, open pan layer the following:

6 medium fish fillets, cut into 2-inch squares

3 lbs. of freshly peeled medium shrimp

1 pt. fresh oysters seasoned with:

1 Tbsp. garlic paste

½ tsp. black pepper

½ tsp. celery salt

½ tsp. tarragon

Top with 1 large diced onion, ½ cup diced celery, and 1 large green bell pepper cut in strips. Place several slices of fresh ripe tomato on top. Sprinkle with paprika. Place uncovered in a 300° preheated oven and cook until tomato slices collapse. Remove from oven, and let stand for 30 minutes. Serve over fresh rice.

Cajun Seafood Gumbo

Serves 6

Heat 1 gallon of water to a boil.

Dice 1 onion, 4 sticks of celery, 1 bell pepper.

Begin preparing roux. Heat ½ cup vegetable oil in iron skillet. Add ½ to 1 cup flour (until it's loose). Stir over a medium fire until it is very brown *but not burned.* Add diced onion, celery, and green pepper. Stir, adding a little hot water until mixture is very brown *but not burned.*

Empty the contents into the pot of hot water. Then, add the following ingredients to the pot:

1 16 oz. can whole tomatoes

1 small bunch chopped green onions

1 Tbsp. garlic paste (lightly salted)

4 fish fillets, cut small

6 fresh, clean crabs

2 lbs. fresh, cleaned medium shrimp

½ tsp. black pepper

¼ tsp. cayenne pepper

Simmer 3 to 4 hours, then add 1 pint of fresh oysters. Simmer for 30 minutes and add 1 Tbsp. of gumbo fillet. Stir and let stand for 30 minutes. Pour over rice and serve.

Fried Fish, Shrimp, and Oysters—Cooked the Old-fashioned Way

(I recommend peanut oil for this recipe, but vegetable oil can be used as well.) Heat oil in a deep skillet. Drop match in oil. When match lights, oil is ready for cooking. Roll clean fish fillets, shrimp, and oysters in a 1-to-1 mixture of cornmeal and flour.

To fry fish, drop in hot oil and brown. Drain and serve. Fry shrimp same as fish. Drain and serve. To fry oysters, drop in hot oil. When cornmeal browns on one side, flip. This usually takes ½ minute or less. Drain and serve. Be careful not to over cook.

Fried Hard-shell Crabs

(Estimate how many crabs per person)

Open crabs and clean. Wash crabs and place shells in a line.

Separate and crack crab claws for easier eating and for seasoning.

Season with celery salt and sprinkle lightly with paprika, salt, and black pepper.

Stuff crab full of a 1-to-1 corn meal and flour mix or ready-mix fish fry.

Heat peanut or vegetable oil in large iron skillet.

Place crabs into hot grease (shell down). The shell itself will cook the meat almost immediately. Cook about ½ minute on each side. Do not overcook.

Roll crab claws in cornmeal and flour mixture and drop in same grease for no longer than 1 minute. The meat comes out easier when fried and tastes much richer. Drain and serve.

Spanish Mackerel

Fried

(Estimate one mackerel per person)

Cut fish in 2-inch squares. Marinate in vinegar and vegetable oil for 30 minutes.

Drain and season with: black pepper and garlic paste.

Dip mackerel in egg batter. Roll in a 1-to-1 cornmeal and flour mix.

Brown on both sides in hot peanut oil.

Drain and serve.

Broiled

Serves 4–6

Marinate four large, skinned fillets in vinegar and oil for 30 minutes. Drain, and place in an open pan with ¼ lb. pure butter, melted. Season liberally with garlic paste and pepper. Sprinkle with paprika, and place a slice of fresh tomato on each fillet. Top with several strips of bell pepper. Broil in 250° preheated oven until tomatoes and peppers are soft. Baste with butter and lemon juice. Don't overcook!

Fried Bluefish

(Estimate 1 blue fish per person}

Cut *fresh* fish into finger-size strips.

Season with: Black pepper and garlic paste.

Dip in egg batter. Roll in 1-to-1 cornmeal and flour mix.

Fry *very* brown on both sides.

Drain and serve.

Seafood Stew

Serves 8

½ cup oil

6 Tbsp. flour

1 large onion, finely chopped

1 large bell pepper, finely chopped

1 shallot, chopped

2 large potatoes, cubed

1 cup shrimp

1 cup crab meat

4 fish fillets, cut in cubes

Warm oil in a large iron pot, then stir in flour. When the flour is dark brown, add the rest of the ingredients. Cover and smother over a low fire about 15 minutes. Fill pot about half full of water and cook about 45 minutes or until potatoes are tender.

Add seafood, and simmer another 15 minutes. Serve over rice.

Venison Leg Roast (Tender and Juicy)

Serves 8–10

Wash a venison leg roast with warm water and marinate in pure vinegar 2 to 3 hours. Drain and cut several slots on both sides. Fill slots with beef suet or pork fat.

Rub fresh garlic paste and plenty of black pepper over the roast and sprinkle with paprika or red pepper.

Quarter 2 onions and 2 large potatoes, place around roast.

Bake covered for 3 hours in 350° oven, adding water when needed. Cut temperature down to 265° and bake until the leg bone is exposed.

Cool, and slice thin.

Wild Duck—Cooked the Old-fashioned Way

(1 duck per person)

Pick ducks clean. Wash and marinate overnight in a 1-to-1 vinegar-water mix.

The next day, drain and season with fresh garlic paste and black pepper.

Fill ducks with bread dressing and place in a large, covered roaster with 4 apples and 4 large potatoes quartered around the ducks.

Bake in 350° oven for 3 hours. Add water as needed. Cook until tender.

Serve with wild rice, green vegetable, and buttered French bread.

Quail Breasts

(Prepare 18 quail for 6 people)

Wash quail in warm water, marinate in a 1-to-1 vinegar-vegetable oil mix for 1 to 2 hours.

Drain and season each with:

½ tsp. celery salt

½ tsp. black pepper

sprinkle with garlic

Brown quail on all sides in hot vegetable oil in a large iron skillet. Place quail, breast side up, in the skillet. Add a large, diced onion and a small amount of water. Cover skillet and cook over a medium-low fire until tender. Add water as needed.

Duck Gumbo

Serves 6

Cut six duck breasts into cubes. Roll in flour, and brown in skillet.

Follow directions for Cajun Seafood Gumbo. For flavor, add 4 small fish fillets.

Place browned duck in gumbo pot already in progress. Simmer over low fire 4 to 5 hours until meat is very tender. One pint of oysters can be added the last 30 minutes for flavor. Let gumbo stand one hour. Serve over rice and with buttered French garlic bread.

Dry Beans (Red or Pinto)

Serves 6

Wash and soak 1½ pounds of dry beans overnight. Boil approximately 3 pounds of ham hocks and ½ pound of salt pork until tender. Add beans and the following:

1 large, cut onion

1 small bunch of chopped green onions

1 large green bell pepper, cut in strips

1 Tbsp. garlic paste

1 tsp. black pepper

Cover, and cook in iron pot over a medium fire for 3 hours. Add water as needed. Serve over rice.

Hot Matagorda Bay

Dene Grigar, the Plugger's youngest daughter

Quivering, glistening, milkywhite creature with some small spot of
  black
gristle, stretching out, live on a bumpy gray shell. This thing,
Quivering again, he holds out to me, its thick, watery juice
leaking off the edge onto my hand holding it,
he pushing it towards me, chuckling, taking his knife
with blunt point slits the corner of another, slits the shell of the creature
Quivering inside. He slurps it, wipes his mouth with the back of his
  hand,
exclaims, "This Is Great !," while I keep holding mine thinking—if I
  don't eat this
he will leave me home, won't take me to the reefs anymore, no more
  fishing
with him, no more fishing at all, if I let him down, not eating this thing,
Quivering lying in its shell.

So I watch him—how he eats it, looks so easy, just close my eyes and
  slurp it, wipe my mouth with the back of my hand, exclaim, "This Is
  Great !" chuckle, lie a little.
Just slurp it with my eyes closed so I won't see it quivering, this once, it
  can't hurt, can't be all bad. Why would he be doing this, eating this
  thing, if it was bad?

So I hold it closer to my mouth, smelling it now with my eyes closed
  hoping not to see the milkywhite ball, its spot of black gristle, the
  bumpy gray shell. With my eyes closed I sniff at it—salt, dead fish,
  seaweed. Doesn't smell milkywhite, white smells clean; this creature
  smells brown, like brown, gray, oily water of hot Matagorda Bay,
  quivering thickly, rankly like this with its black gristle and its
  bumpy gray shell.

So I quit breathing for a minute not to smell this thing in its shell, with
  my eyes closed to quit seeing it quivering, while trying to push it
  nearer to my mouth, then feeling this thing leak thick juice on my
  hand, it touching me, and I swear I hear it moving, sliding backward
  on its shell wanting me not to eat it, not to slurp it down.

So I open my eyes for a second, peeking at my father cracking open
another, me getting behind by this time knowing he will notice me
not eating—me needing to slurp loudly, wipe my mouth with the
back of my hand, exclaim,—"This Is Good ?" Both of us crouching
on the reef of shells of creatures in the hot Matagorda Bay, he having
the time of his life slitting open little creatures with the blunt point of
his knife, slurping one at a time while I work hard to get down my
first, my one quivering one, knowing full well I have to eat it or not
come fishing with him again.

So I grip the edges of the shell tighter, clamp my eyes shut again, and
turn the shell over into my mouth—down my throat it slides
quivering all the way down before I have a chance to chew, it
happening so fast, me not knowing if I was supposed to chew or just
simply swallow the whole thing all at once gagging like I'm doing,
then swallowing, gasping, breathing again, opening my eyes,
looking at my father, remembering me forgetting to slurp, wipe my
mouth with the back of my hand, exclaim, "This Is Disgusting!" just
it sliding down and me gagging and trying to breathe.

So I see my father watching me, roaring laughing, beaming at me,
feeling him slapping me on my shoulder, pulling my cap down over
my eyes, calling me Sport, slapping me again. I totter over onto the
shells, sprawling out over them, quivering, laughing with him,
asking for another. This time I won't forget, won't forget to slurp, to
wipe my mouth with the back of my hand, exclaim "How Incredibly
Great This All Is !"— the reef, my father, me, the hot Matagorda Bay.

February 1994

Plugger

192

Index

A

C

D

Gulf Coast Conservation
Association (GCCA), 2,
82 - 3, 86, 111
Gulf flounder, *See fish*
Gulfport, 2, 122
gulls, 5, 37, 63, 124, 128, 181
gumbo, 182, 185, 190

H

Hagen, Ken, 70 -71
Halls Lakes, 96
Hanna's Reef, 22 - 3, 30, 32, 137
hardware fishermen, 15, 17
hatcheries, 83, 92
Hauser, Ron, 67
Hawkins, Elmer, 1, 17, 20
Helton Boat Works, 114
Hermann Park Lake, 141
Hollowood Bayou, 65
honey hole, 4, 15, 105, 130,
132 - 3, 135
hooks:
Eagle Claw,® 151, 163 - 4
multi, 32
single, 29, 32, 47, 130,
144, 150 - 1, 161, 163,
167
snelled, 163
treble, 15, 145, 151, 161,
163
Hopedale, Louisiana, 74, 121
Hopkins, Buzz, 15
Horseshoe Lake, 96

houseboat: *Plugger*, 3, 70 - 1,
75, 130, 133, 181
Houston, 1, 9, 13, 17, 19, 24 - 5,
46 - 7, 51 - 4, 65, 67, 70, 83,
97 - 8, 114, 141, 150
Houston Angler's Club, 141
Houston Chronicle, 24, 36, 150
Houston Post, 24
Houston Press, 24
Houston Ship Channel, 110
Hudson Engineering Com-
pany, 52
hurricane:
Beulah, 91
Bob, 69
Claudette, 68
Frederick, 3, 61, 69 - 70,
72

I

ice:
block, 46, 181
dry, 46
inflatable boat, 57
Intracoastal Waterway, 41, 50,
88 - 90, 92, 98

J

Jamaica Beach Development,
34
Japan, 139
jellyfish, 147
Jimmy's Duck Hunting Lodge,
15

Paradoski, Charlie, 55
Pascagola, Mississippi, 70
Payne, Ed, 50
Pelican Lake, 97
Peterson's Fishing Camp, 28
Pettus, Texas, 4
Pluggin' Shorty, *See Stettner*
pollution, 10, 88, 91, 96 - 9, 175
Port Aransas, Texas, 14
Port Isabel Bay, 89
Port Lavaca, Texas, 106
Port Mansfield, Texas, 89,
    110, 157
Port O'Connor, Texas, 29, 37,
    40, 50 - 1, 56 - 7, 69, 92, 98,
    104, 106, 115, 131, 157
Pringle Lake, 57
Prudhomme, Paul, 80 - 1

Q

Quail Breasts, 189

R

redfish, *See fish*
    rat reds, *See fish*
red snapper, *See fish*
Red Windmill, 132
reels:
    Ambassadeur 4500C, B,
        140
    Ambassadeur 5000, 139
    Ambassadeur 5500C, 140
    Garcia, 139

Garcia 5500 Delux Gold-
    Plated, 140
Langly, 139
Quantum 600T.L. Low
    Profile, 140
Shimano Pro Bantam, 140
Shimano Bantam Mag, 140
South Bend 60, 139
Sportscast, 139
Reynolds, Harry, 1
Riding, Joe, 1
Robinson Bayou, 96
Rockport, Texas, 14 - 5, 115,
    159, 178
Rohan, August, 11
Rohan, Gus, 12
Rosenberg, Texas, 10
Rosharon, Texas, 12

S

San Antonio Bay, 42, 51, 53 - 4,
    97, 137
San Bernard River, 9, 97
San Fernando, 44
San Luis Pass, 19, 25 - 7, 38 - 9,
    108
Schooner Harbor, 133
Schumacher, Doctor, 60
Schutte, Richard, 67
Schwartz, Carl, 53 - 4
Scooter boats, 115
Seadrift, Texas, 118
Seafood a la Chandeleur, 185
Seafood Stew, 188
Seal, Buddy, 62, 67

Sealy, Texas, 103
sea trout, *See fish*
Shakespeare Tackle Company,
139, 141
sharks, *See fish*
Shell Beach, Louisiana, 70, 71
Shell Island, 138
SiloFlex, 142
skiff, 4, 42, 44 - 5, 114, 119 - 21,
131
skipjack, *See fish*
Slaten, Stan, 24 - 5, 149 - 50
Slidell, Louisiana, 3, 70
snook, *See fish*
Soto la Marina, Mexico, 42,
44, 46
Soto la Marina River, 175
South Bend Tackle Company,
139
South Lake, 54
Spanish mackerel, *See fish*
speckled trout, *See fish*
Stettner, Anton "Pluggin'
Shorty," 1, 15, 160
stingrays, *See fish*
Stockton, Curtis, 44
Sugarland, Texas, 12

T

Taliaferro, Zollie, 1, 17, 35, 43,
90, 142
tarpon, *See fish*
Taylor Lake, 96
telephoning, 105

Texas City, 30
Texas City Hurricane Protection Dike, 96
trout, *See fish*
Turtle Bayou, 96, 178

V

Venison Leg Roast, 189
Victoria Canal, 97
Vincent, Al, 52, 71

W

Waddell, Bill, 103
Walker, Bill, 24
Wallis, 9
Wasicek, Walter, 13
Webb, Jerry, 69
Well Runner, 121
West Bay, 24 - 5, 29 - 30
West Columbia, Texas, 12
Wild Duck, 189
Wortham, Bill, 29 - 30, 50

Y

Yakapoo, 71 - 2, 74 - 5
Yarborough Pass, 89

Z

Zipprian Bayou, 96 - 7